Google Apps for Education

Building Knowledge in a Safe and Free Environment

Roger Nevin
Micah Melton
David V. Loertscher

Hi Willow Research and Publishing
November, 2011

Content current through Dec. 13, 2010

Hi Willow Research and Publishing
312 South 1000 East
Salt Lake City UT 84102

Distributed by:
LMC Source
P.O. Box 131266
Spring TX 77393
800-873-3043
sales@lmcsource.com

ISBN: 978-1-933170-63-3

ebook editions available from Amazon.com and Barnes and Noble

Table of Contents

Introduction

In response to the many fears that the growing access to the Internet by the children and young people of North America was causing harm, even dangers, Google has created a suite of tools that every school can use in a protected, safe, and free environment.

In this book, we introduce the developing tool suite for schools and school districts considering the possibilities, but we also have a larger purpose in mind.

Google Apps for Education is more than a few tools that open up some efficiencies; it is an entire revolution in teaching and learning. Yes, many opportunities for personal and collaborative efficiencies are opened such as tools that are simple to use and available on almost any computing device, anywhere, and at any time, but there is more.

Suddenly as everyone has access to cloud computing 24/7 and the tools allow for collaborative construction of documents, video, websites, wikis, and more, a transformation from top-down education suddenly opens to constructivist spaces where teachers, specialists, administrators, experts, and parents are coaches and the learners can begin to take command of their own learning. It is not an evolutionary occurrence. It is revolutionary.

While we concentrate here on introducing briefly the array of tools that form the suite, our real purpose is to explore the possibilities of a revolutionary education enabled by this tool package. We introduce the idea of a physical and virtual learning commons in the school that combines the library and computer labs with Google Apps for Education as a foundational element. We introduce the idea of knowledge building centers where adult coaches and students are working collaboratively on high-level learning experiences where critical thinking, creative thinking, habits of mind, collaborative intelligence, and metacognitive experiences transforms end engages learners. We regularly suggest ideas where the tools turn transparent and the focus of a project is on creating deep understanding and learning how to learn rather than struggle with a technology that may or may not work.

And we are constantly mindful of the difficulties many schools are having embracing a technology that is more open than closed to a technology that confronts the fears that many have and renders those fears groundless. Thus, in part three, we tackle some of the issues that administrators and tech directors are likely to face as they adopt and enable Google Apps for Education.

As this book comes into print and as an ebook, we are mindful that we have a moving target as a topic. Google is constantly working to improve the entire suite of tools they offer and keep adding new tools and features. Thus, we have created both a website and a Facebook page in an attempt to create a discussion and updating of the tools. You can find these resources at:

Webpage: getgoogleapps.com
Facebook page: http://www.facebook.com/GoogleAppsForEdBuildingKnowledge

We invite our readers to participate in this conversation, ask questions, and to answer questions and share experiences with others who are wanting to, implementing, or are already on the road of successful implementation.

Google offers a variety of venues in support of persons using Google Apps for Education and while we cite some of those helps, we encourage our readers to discover and share those helps as they become available. Google often exhibits at conferences where they provide wonderful demonstrations and counseling. They also provide seminars and certify teachers if you are lucky enough to apply minutes after registration opens.

Our concern is that the suite of tools offered might be underutilized as a way of "automating" what already goes on in a regular classroom. That is, we are afraid that many teachers might just duplicate their assignments from a paper world into a virtual world. There is nothing more disastrous, in our opinion, of using and doing the same old, same old methods in this innovative environment. To do so is to demonstrate the idea that "we have used technology and it doesn't make any difference."

So, as we introduce the tools and the ideas for transformation, we encourage our readers to experiment, share, collaborate, and transform learning experiences that will enable a true 21st Century education and prepare this tech-savvy generation for the global world already upon us. And we appreciate individual and collective feedback and suggestions:

Roger Nevin: rnevin@gmail.com
Michah Melton: mr.m.melton@gmail.com
David Loertscher: reader.david@gmail.com

Part I

Google Apps for Education as a Knowledge Building Environment

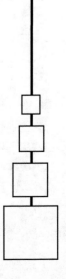

Chapter 1

Web 2.0—It's all About Improved
Teaching, Learning, and Knowledge Building

The Problem

Today's students are generally eager and enthusiastic about working with technology. Their teachers, on the other hand, are more of a mixed bag. Some educators are very comfortable integrating collaborative learning technologies into their lessons and recognize the merits of doing so, while some others seem unwilling or unable to do the same, despite research showing the benefit to students.

A review of the literature shows the recognized value of collaborative learning as well as the challenges and demands today's students present in educational settings (Breeding, 2006; Chu, Chow, Tse & Kihlthau, 2008; Gokhale, 1995; Saxton, 2008; Simpson, 2007; Vygotsky, 1978). New technologies exist to facilitate collaborative learning on a scale never before possible and in ways that better engage today's students (Fredrick, 2008; Gersh, 2009; Rosenfeld, 2008; Saxton, 2008). Still, despite growing evidence that incorporating new collaborative learning technologies into curricula would likely mean increased student engagement, increased student achievement, and increased productivity all around, many of today's teachers seem reluctant to do so for a variety of reasons. If this reluctance could be overcome, students would likely benefit.

In the U.S. National Technology Plan, 2010, the objective is very clear: "Just as technology is at the core of virtually every aspect of our daily lives and work, we must leverage it to provide engaging and powerful learning experiences, content, and resources and assessments that measure student achievement in more complete, authentic, and meaningful ways. Technology-based learning and assessment systems will be pivotal in improving student learning and generating data that can be used to continuously improve the education system at all levels. Technology will help us execute collaborative teaching strategies combined with professional learning that better prepare and enhance educators' competencies and expertise over the course of their careers. To shorten our learning curve, we can learn from other kinds of enterprises that have used technology to improve outcomes while increasing productivity."

Contemporary Students' Needs & Characteristics

The world of today's students is markedly different from the one most of their teachers knew as adolescents. While many of the issues today's students face remain the same (e.g., struggles with authority, independence, self-identity, etc.), the ways they experience the world, access information and interact with one another have changed in ways unimaginable to their forebears. Revolutionary developments in information technology over the last decades have been the primary cause of these changes, and the fruits of these developments affect almost all aspects of our daily lives.

Most of today's teachers grew up in a world in which the information technologies of today were just emerging or beginning to take root. A consequence of this is that many teachers seem to underestimate the utility of the current generation of information technology or overestimate the difficulty of learning to utilize it.

Today's students, however, hail from a world in which this incredible technology is taken for granted. For these students, the Internet and other technologies have always existed and they have come to expect their incorporation into the curriculum. Technologies like Google Docs (a free, online word processing, presentation, and spreadsheet application with features that enable almost instantaneous collaboration from remote locations) offer educators opportunities to engage students in collaborative learning experiences never before possible.

Web 2.0: What and Why?

As collaborative learning techniques evolve, so too do the technologies available to facilitate these techniques. This growing array of revolutionary new collaborative tools —dubbed Web 2.0—includes tools such as Google Docs, which enables users to easily create and share information and ideas instantly and electronically. After years working as an Associate Professor of Educational Computing at New York State College at Buffalo, Thompson (2008) reported that the incorporation of these new tools into educators' curricula is causing a significant shift "from individualized work to collaborative efforts, from individual learning to collective knowledge, from passive to active creation" (p. 11).

This shift from individual to collaborative learning is being enthusiastically received by students accustomed to working with Web 2.0 technologies. The incredible popularity of social networking sites like Facebook and Twitter are but two examples of how the more interactive nature of Web 2.0 technologies appeals to Millennials (according to Breeding, 2006, those born between 1981 and 2000). These students are not only comfortable using these technologies, but they are also demanding their inclusion (Gersh, 2009). Put simply, these students expect their learning to be digital. After all, their lives outside of school are immersed in technology (e.g., "smart" cell phones, iPods, instant messaging, video game consoles, etc.), so educators should not be surprised when they express their reluctance to learn solely via pencil, paper, and textbook.

The new possibilities engendered by Web 2.0 applications like Google Docs are not merely relegated to student productivity alone, but can also provide educators with tremendous resources to collaborate with their students and one another. Saxton (2008) provided an overview on the use of blogs (weblogs), RSS (Really Simple Syndication) feeds, wikis, Google Docs and other emerging applications as valuable tools in educators' professional development. In her overview, Saxton described the ease of collaboration these new technologies make possible and expressed her excitement at developments and implementations to come (p. 27). Saxton encouraged educators to experiment with Web 2.0 technologies, but advised starting slow to build confidence and avoid frustration.

Google Apps for Education

To date, the world of Web 2.0 has been a giant shopping bag of tools with various advocates creating lists of the best, arguing their brands at conferences, and publicizing their ideas on blogs, in periodicals and in books. Now, both Google and Microsoft have created worlds, safe environments, or umbrella spaces in which a class or a school can enjoy a variety of Web 2.0 tools in a suite. With their ease of use and friendly interfaces, these suites are likely to boost the use of Web 2.0 faster than the shopping bag approach of the past. This is certainly true for both students and their teachers, and, in particular, the administrators and IT directors who have historically been uneasy to extend computing into the cloud for fear of losing control. All said, we are probably witnessing a revolution in the instructional use of technology as the utility of these tools becomes undeniable and the choice to ignore them becomes unfathomable.

References

Breeding, M. (2006). Technology for the next generation. *Computers in Libraries*, 26(10), 28-30.

Chu, S., Chow, K., Tse, S., & Kihlthau, C. (2008). Grade 4 students' development of research skills through inquiry-based learning projects. *School Libraries Worldwide*, 14 (1), 10-37.

Fredrick, K. (2008). A gaggle of goodies from Google (cover story). *School Library* Media Activities Monthly, 25(4), 44-46.

Gersh, S. (2009). Global projects and digital tools. *MultiMedia & Internet@Schools*, 16(1), 10-13.

Gokhale, A. (1995). Collaborative learning enhances critical thinking. *Journal of Technology Education*, 7(1), 22-30.

National Technology Plan: *Transforming American Education: Learning Powered by Technology*, 2010 at: http://www.ed.gov/technology/netp-2010 (quote from the Executive Summary, p. 3).

Rosenfeld, B. (2008). The challenges of teaching with technology: From computer idiocy to computer competence. International Journal of Instructional Media, 35(2), 157-166.

Rosenfeld, E. (2008). Useful Web 2.0 tools for teachers and students. *Teacher Librarian*, 35 (4), 72.

Saxton, B. (2008). Information tools: using blogs, RSS, and wikis as professional resources. *Young Adult Library Services*, 6(2), 27-29.

Simpson, C. (2007). From immigrant to native. *Library Media Connection*, 25(4), 6.

Thompson, J. (2008). Don't be afraid to explore Web 2.0. Education Digest, 74(4), 19-22.

Vygotsky, L.S. (1978). *Mind and society: The development of higher psychological processes. Cambridge, MA: Harvard University Press.*

Other Research Studies:

- *SIIA: Results of the Spring 2010 SIIA Vision K-20 Survey: Technology – Education – America's Future.* SIIA, June 29, 2010. Full link: http://www.siia.net/index.php? option=com_docman&task=doc_download&Itemid=318&gid=2634
  This research study done by the Software & Information Industry Association shows that from 2008-2010, only very slow progress has been made in the integration of technology into teaching and learning.

- The Walden University 2010 study: "Educators, Technology and 21st Century Skills: Dispelling Five Myths" paints a bit better picture of technology adoption on a wider scale: http://www.waldenu.edu/Degree-Programs/Masters/ 36427.htm

Chapter 2

Google Apps for Education

Prelude: What is cloud computing?

Before we even introduce Google Apps for Education, we need to discuss cloud computing. When most schools began to build networks for technology, each district created or purchased systems that were stand-alone and local. That meant that all data and information was stored on local storage systems and was usually controlled by a single person or very small group of individuals. However, email systems (notably Gmail) began to develop server farms where the actual messages were not stored locally but elsewhere and backed up someplace else. This provided all of us access wherever, whenever, and from whatever device we happened to use. Thus, we say our email messages are stored in the "cloud"—somewhere out there in the great beyond of server farms. Before long, cloud computing became so popular and reliable that it was just a matter of time before the great migration for all kinds of data and information began to occur.

To tech directors and others used to having absolute power and control over every aspect of hardware, software, and information, the cloud seemed a major threat to control and safety. For those in Canada, the fact that the server farms were located in the U.S. stoked fears that the U.S. Patriot Act might interfere with information in unacceptable ways.

As the trend toward cloud computing grew exponentially with fewer and fewer problems, anxieties and fears lessened. At the time of this writing, there is a major trend by schools and school districts across the continent to utilize the much cheaper solution of cloud computing and concentrate at the local level to increase accessibility and bandwidth. Much of this is in response to the explosive availability of wireless computing devices, which has lead to both teachers and students demanding more and more access wherever and whenever they choose. We expect no lessening of this demand over the next few years and feel confident that cloud computing is here to stay.

The 2009 Horizon Report predicted that "six emerging technologies or practices ... are likely to enter mainstream use in learning-focused organizations within three adoption horizons over the next one to five years." According to leading experts in education, the two most important trends in education for the next coming years in technology are cloud computing and portability.

Enter Google Apps and Google Apps for Education

Soon after Google's introduction of Gmail, they began to build apps that could be used freely by anyone, anywhere. Various apps (applications) such as Google Documents and Google Spreadsheets appeared and gained popularity as an alternative to software packages such as Microsoft Office. These apps were free and worked whether you owned a PC or a Mac. In popular usage, apps became a common term: There is an app for this and an app for that as every iPhone and iPad or Android device user knows.

Google envisioned a system for children and teens in the world of education that would begin to alleviate the growing criticism they were hearing about the unsafe world of the Internet. Their idea was to gather a group of their apps that were already freely available to everyone and create individualized environments that schools, districts, and states could use in a protected environment. Unfortunately, they named this product Google Apps for Education rather than a name that would distinguish this product from the general world of apps. Thus, if you ask someone, "Are you using Google Apps for Education?" they are likely to confuse general apps with this specific product.

Throughout this book, we try to use the entire name, Google Apps for Education, because there are differences in the different applications whether you are using the public version of the product or the one inside the protected Google Apps for Education environment. It is a bit annoying but necessary to make the distinction. Occasionally, we lapse into the shorter version we title Google Apps rather than the generic Google apps.

The package Google has created for schools is a safe and free environment and they have promised that this environment will always remain free (something we doubt, but hope they honor over time). The family of tools under this safe environment is constantly growing and developing. Thus, any book on the topic is out of date the moment it is issued. For example, we thought our task was virtually complete when Google suddenly announced in late Nov. 2010 that over 50 new apps would be available for Google Apps for Education. That is why the authors have created a website (getgoogleapps.com) and a Facebook page to accompany this publication, so that in between editions, if the market warrants further attention, we can respond to the changing landscape. The Facebook page is at: http://www.facebook.com/GoogleAppsForEdBuildingKnowledge

Google Apps for Education

As it exists currently, Google Apps for Education is a suite of tools in a closed environment managed by an administrator in each school or district. These tools can be turned on or off at the discretion of the administrator. We have created chapters for this book on a number of basic tools within the suite that are potentials for the administrator to open. Once the administrator applies to Google for permission, the various tools can be opened up and at that point, the administrator "opens" the cloud to students and teachers for access 24/7 from any location and on most school or personal devices. Thus, at that point, a whole new environment is available and the entire potential for and impact on teaching and learning is enabled. More details about how this is accomplished is covered in the last part of this book.

As the entire suite of tools are turned on, a new world of possibilities emerges. Our purpose is to introduce some of the basics but also some of the vision that doesn't occur to basic users with just a working knowledge of the tools.

We recommend the adoption of Google Apps for Education because we believe that it fulfills the following criteria of any technological tool adoption:
- it must improve learning
- it must engage students
- it must be based on best practices and research
- it is free (if possible) and sustainable
- it has been tested and successfully implemented in a variety of settings
- students can use the technology both at home and school
- cloud solutions are preferred (entire application runs through a browser) portable devices are preferred (netbooks / PDAs)

As we all build experience in this new environment alongside our students, we can first realize the many efficiencies that the various tools offer and the availability of those tools both in school and out. But if the recommendations of the following chapters are realized, quite a different environment arises. We have encouraged tech directors, teacher librarians, and classroom teachers to keep a log of the changes and impact on teaching and learning as it changes over time.
- What was it like before the Google Apps environment became a reality?
- What began to change as students and teachers went to a 24/7 safe and free environment?
- What teaching practices began to change?
- What changes did we see in the engagement of learners and the progress in deep understanding and learning how to learn through technology?
- What challenges arose and how were they resolved?
- What changed for teacher technologists, teacher librarians, other specialists in the school, parents, and classroom teachers?

Let the journey begin.

References

In his "The Scaling Framework" published by Microsoft, Chris Dede of Harvard describes how innovation must happen in education and how technology can contribute to that shift. http://www.microsoft.com/education/demos/scale/

Chapter 3

Google Apps as the Central Feature of the Virtual Learning Commons

Using Google Apps either separately or within the environment of Google Apps Education can be a part of an organization within the school known as the Learning Commons. A Learning Commons is a merger between the school library and computer labs of the school and where all the specialists of the school make their services available to the entire faculty and student body.

The Learning Commons has both a physical space and a virtual space that has a Wikipedia-type feel. That is, the Learning Commons is not a place adults build for others to come, it is a place the users build, construct, share, and contribute to.

In the **Physical Learning Commons**, book stacks and banks of computers are moved out from the center of the room so that many different kinds of flexible learning spaces can happen. Multiple groups can be meeting, working, learning, performing, studying, and producing as part of various learning activities across the school. The specialists of the schools are working alongside the classroom teachers in the Learning Commons and a sense of ownership by the clients is very evident. The wireless environment allows various configurations of computing devices connected to cloud computing networks.

In the **Virtual Learning Commons**, the former school library website is replaced by a collaborative digital environment, again built by everyone. It is not only the home of a digital catalog of resources but is the collaborative center of projects, school culture, and collaborative learning experiences. In this virtual and collaborative digital environment, Google Apps for Education is the perfect foundational element of collaboration. It stands at the center, since by definition it is a collaborative and constructivist environment filled with tools that make collaboration a natural.

Other features of the Virtual Learning Commons include a virtual school yearbook, virtual book clubs, projects happening across classes or schools or across the world, the place where school culture and achievements including sports events are being loaded and distributed, and above all, a place that has many contributors from students to teachers, to teacher librarians, to parents, and to administrators. It is the "Wikipedia" of the entire school culture.

Of the many features that could be a part of a Virtual Learning Commons, a simple but transforming tool becomes a central element that we call Knowledge Building Centers. These are environments of learning units created using a template in Google Sites as

pictured below.

Instead of the classroom teacher being alone and creating isolated assignments, adults, specialists, classroom teachers, administrators, experts, and parents are building knowledge and learning how to learn skills together. (More about how Knowledge Building Centers work is contained in chapters 5 and 12 of this book.)

Google Apps for Education replaces many very expensive course management systems; however, at the moment it lacks a tool teachers can use to assess and grade student work (though gradebooks can be easily created). With a bit of practice and a good gradebook software program, teachers can go paperless. There is no other step forward that will change a teacher's work world and the world of collaboration more than going paperless. Among the many advantages:

- Keeping organized with a massive number of student responses to various projects and assignments.
- Being able to assess anywhere at any time as long as one is connected.
- Being able to communicate instantly with students about problems, suggestions and the results of assessments. This is true of individual students, small groups, and whole classes.
- Being able to receive student work from anywhere at anytime.

- The ability to be connected to projects as they are in progress, to watch who, when, and how students are participating and being able to monitor, coach, assess, and contribute throughout a project in real time. This real time monitoring of learning is just not possible in the physical world. Teachers and specialists who are participating virtually, either in a totally online learning experience or a face-to-face one, discover that they can be more effective and efficient, saving time for both students and themselves when individuals or small groups get off on the wrong track.
- And, its green.

The Learning Commons approach to school culture transforms a series of isolated teaching pods into a true collaborative school experience where everyone can work toward a common goal. It is a major departure from 20th century schooling practices when everyone "gets it" and understands the foundational vision at work. In the literature, this transformation is called a threshold concept—an experience or portal through which one goes never to go back to previously held beliefs.

Resources

(available from LMC Source at: http://lmcsource.com)
- *The New Learning Commons Where Learners Win! Reinventing School Libraries and Computer Labs* by David V. Loertscher, Carol Koechlin and Sandi Zwaan; ISBN: 978-1-933170-40-4; Hi Willow Research and Publsihing; 2008.
- *Building a Learning Commons* by Carol Koechlin, Esther Rosenfeld, and David V. Loertscher; Hi Willow Research and Publishing; ISBN: 978-1-933170-59-6; 2010.
- *Learning Commons Treasury* by David V. Loertscher and Elizabeth "Betty" Marcoux, eds.; Teacher Librarian Press; 2010; ISBN: 978-1-61751-000-7.
- *The Big Think: 9 Metacognative Stratagies That Make the End Just the Beginning of Learning* by David V. Loertscher, Carol Koechlin, and Sandi Zwaan; Hi Willow Research and Publishing; 2009; ISBN 978-1-933170-45-9.

Chapter 4

The Advantages of Google Apps for Education

Every school, school district, school board, or other organizational configuration is scanning the horizon for new and better ways to educate the current and future generations with a more affordable model. In this chapter, we cover three major advantages the Google Apps for Education provides to the school community.

Students Need to Learn Cloud Computing to Compete in the Global Economy

Students are more likely than not to already be a part of various social networks such as Facebook and certainly use their cell phones for an increasingly number of applications such as texting, scanning websites, playing games, watching YouTube, and reading eBooks. Google Apps allows this familiarity with cloud computing to slide into the world of academia using Google Apps for Education without a great deal of training. They are already acquainted with the concept of anywhere, anytime access to tools, friends, and functions that keep them connected.

In accessing applications beyond social networks, students are joining a trend worldwide as they blend their social and academic lives to develop personal learning networks. In these networks, each student is both teacher, learner, participant, activist, creator, and problem solver, and each is generally connected.

Businesses, colleges and universities are moving towards cloud computing. Students who work in the cloud will be working in a "real world" paradigm that will directly give them the skills necessary for post secondary education and work. The cloud allows each student to build a personal portfolio containing both demonstrations of personal expertise and collaborative projects. Employers often "google" prospective employees to find such demonstrations of expertise.

Why Google Apps for Education Makes Administrators Look Good

With the advent of online education, more and more choices are opening up for students of all ages. Administrators who realize this more competitive situation can use environments such as Google Apps for Education to build a brand that signals progressive ideas and opportunities worth considering by prospective clients.

Even within a small community that values a local brick and mortar school as the center of sports, community identity, and pride, online opportunities for individual students and groups provide the best of both worlds. For example, in one small school district in very rural Utah, students have the option of face-to-face or online attendance. This has proven advantageous as students utilizing the online option graduate at the same rate and in the same time frame as their more traditional counterparts. If urban schools and others were to follow this diversified model, they too could provide the advantages of magnet schools with their specialization alongside the more generalized pathway.

By gaining the experience of Knowledge Building Centers as a part of Google Apps for Education, a particular "school" can be almost any configuration imaginable and at the same time practical for the kids in a neighborhood or virtual groups across the world. In other words, Google Apps for Education provides that first major step into the cloud and onto the roadway into the future. The wise administrator capitalizes on this progressive stance to attract students and teachers into a vibrant educational experience. Fortunately, more and more funding models are also allowing for such experimentation.

Already, administrators are enticing parents to become a major part of the education of their children in a wide variety of ways not possible before. From face-to-face after school programs to virtual online involvement 24/7, parents are being brought into the fold. By reaching out to experts throughout the world for projects, entire families can become partners in the building of globally competitive learners, doers, creators, and entrepreneurs. The administrator is not only "presiding" over a school but building a personal brand of excellence.

The Advantages and Challenges for IT Coordinators / Systems Administrators

For a number of years, responsibility for technology applications has been given to individual IT coordinators/systems administrators charged by central administrating to provide administrative computing and instructional computing for a district. In turn, many IT coordinators/systems administrators have created intra-district computing environments using very tight controls and overly strict policies across the entire district. With the advent of systems like Google Apps for Education, totally new types of environments are available that offer opportunities but also threats to the "power" of the IT kingdom.

Acceptance of cloud computing where information is stored "out there" rather than on school servers often poses the greatest threats to perceived local control. Questions immediately arise:

- Is it safe?

- What about control?
- Does it meet security standards and requirements?
- What does it cost?
- What will happen to our current systems and employees?

Good and Bad News: Google Apps for Education and cloud computing can save a school district millions of dollars mainly by reducing the cost of and need for IT.

The main argument IT will use for not implementing Google Apps and other cloud computing applications is security and privacy.

Common IT Concerns:
- Security—district school data is maintained outside the district and a third party might access it.
- Privacy—student information can be accessed by a third party.
- Abuse—Email & chat could lead to inappropriate communication between students and sometimes between teacher and students.
- Patriot Act—The United States government can access student and teacher data and use it for prosecution (this is one of the most common excuses in Canada).

Many IT departments are also against open wireless in schools. Wireless is an important component of Google Apps for Education because it allows students much better access from areas of the school that are not computer labs as they bring in their own devices (such as the iPod Touch & iPad) to access Google Apps.

IT's argument for not getting open wireless include:
- Open wireless will lead to viruses infiltrating the board servers.
- Students who use their own equipment will not have the same programs available that are on the school computers (this is not a problem if the school uses Google Apps for Education).
- Students who bring in their own equipment will abuse the system by downloading games and music or watching YouTube. Also students' equipment could be virus infected which could infect the districts' entire network. This argument is actually not true if the open wireless is set up correctly. (Think about all the Starbucks customers who have no problem with viruses even though Starbucks offers free open wireless to all their customers.)
- Students who bring in their own equipment will disrupt classes because they will use the equipment to communicate with each for personal reasons during class time. (The counter argument is that students can use that equipment to collaborate on creative projects with other students.)

Case Study: A school board in Saskatchewan, Canada decided to go wireless and with Google Apps for Education for all students from grades K-12. The feedback from the board was not only that this is a much less expensive option than traditional computer configurations in schools, but more importantly, it improved learning. Such stories are becoming commonplace and the reader can probably find a participating school or school district close by to visit.

As everyone has experienced in the world of technology over the past several decades, one thing is certain: change. At a time when economic factors affect many decisions relating to schooling in general, it is very attractive to encounter a system that can actually save IT departments major expenditures and at the same time open up new opportunities for improved teaching and learning. It is a matter of doing more with less.

"We weighed security concerns against the benefits of flexibility and scalability. After careful analysis of the sensitivity of data, we found the security level provided by the system to be acceptable," said Lim, the head of Singapore's Ministry of Education (MOE) IT department http://blog.mryap.com/why-singapore-schools-chose-the-public-cloud

Chapter 5

Google Apps as a Knowledge Building Environment

One of the major criticisms of using technology in education is that teachers merely transfer paper pencil exercises, lectures, or assignments from one medium to another without any re-examination. Only the delivery mechanism has changed. When this is the case, we cannot expect any improvements in learning, although one could expect a few efficiencies transferring from paper to digital (the dog ate my homework fades as an excuse).

As new technologies and tools have become available, technologists are famous for teaching us all the *potential* benefits of the latest gizmo or software. They dazzle us with possibilities and by the time we have heard the pitch about ten or more new inventions, our heads are swimming with possibilities and excitement, but little more.

For example, we might have a faint notion that a Google document can be collaborative, but unless we test out the power of collaborative writing and editing, we end up with the same batch of individually written reports or essays. If collaborative writing and editing are seriously considered, then the entire assignment must be re-designed to take advantage of that technological innovation. Immediately, new questions arise:
- How do we assess individual work and contribution vs. group creation?
- What do we do with slackers?
- Who is really benefitting from collaborative editing?
- Will collaborative writing and editing help improve what individuals do when they have to write a piece totally on their own?
- Do we assign one grade for the group or can we assign various grades to individual members of a writing team?
- And, what are the actual benefits of collaborative writing?

The Evolutionary Approach

A sound approach in professional development is to begin with a desired improvement to teaching and learning and then consider a variety of tools that could be used to achieve that result. Let us assume that we are seeking ways to improve writing and are convinced that collaborative writing and editing hold some major possibilities. We then investigate a variety of technological tools that have the potential to provide learners a better opportunity and experience. For example, we would reject a typical word processor as compared with a Google document because collaborative, real-time editing is not really possible using the old system. So, various teachers agree to try out collaborative editing with some re-designed assignments and bring the results back to the group for analysis and synthesis.

Teacher technologists and teacher librarians do us a big favor when they build a large repertoire of various tools and then try to match them with the types of teaching and learning strategies that need to be re-examined.

Using the approach outlined here, a faculty might look at an array of challenges that need to be addressed to improve expected results by students. Problem by problem, we then examine the various tools of Google Apps to see if there are tools and techniques for using those tools that might benefit the results we are wanting. As a group, we consider advantages and disadvantages of an array of tools, try various techniques, and then apply those that are producing the best results. It is an on-going experiment because the tools keep evolving and getting better and better. And, in the case of Google Apps, the tools are free.

The Revolutionary Approach

A second approach is to realize that the world of Google Apps is entirely new. We are no longer in a world of direct teaching with a few tools such as a blackboard and some audiovisual equipment for supplementary resources should they be needed to amplify our lectures and demonstrations. Instead, we are in a constructivist world of collaborative teaching and learning. Adults become coaches and students assume the role of team players rather than robot regurgitates. The shift from content and skill mastery to personal excellence leading to collaborative intelligence is awesome to experience for both teachers, specialists, and students if they have been steeped in behaviorists traditions.

This means the instructional design of units is very different. We reinvent the textbook/ lecture/test method into more modern designs such as Understanding by Design and concepts of Differentiation.

Loertscher, Koechlin and Zwaan, builiding upon constructivist principles, have built 18 think models that work very well in the constructivist world of Google Apps. The pattern of these models is to first have individuals or groups build expertise in a topic, problem or quest followed by a mixing of what individuals know in order to build collaborative intelligence. Each model emphasizes the building of content knowledge and a mix of skills needed to acquire that knowledge. The learning experience ends with a Big Think, or metacognitive activity designed to look back at the experience and try to decide how we can all become better in the next one. A sample model appears below:

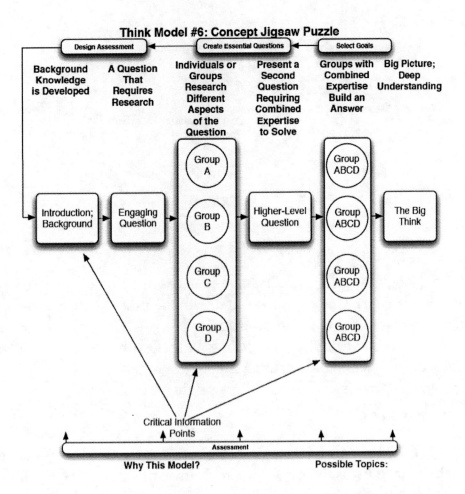

Using the Concept Jigsaw Puzzle Think Model as pictured above, the class might be investigating disasters. Individuals or small groups first study a particular disaster and try to discover how their family could be better prepared to meet that disaster. Usually a learning experience would end here with oral reports by the various groups. Not so in the think models. The groups are jigsawed and given a more difficult challenge to solve. They are to combine the knowledge of the various disaster groups into a plan for their family on how to meet the challenges of any disaster that might strike. At the end and in the Big Think, they might compare what they know about disaster preparedness with an expert invited to the class in person or through Google Talk.

Another way to view the think models is to visualize a world in which the individual student is building personal/group expertise in stage one of the model and then in stage two, building collaborative intelligence as pictured below:

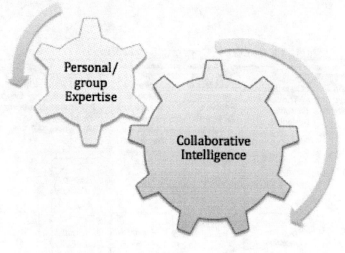

In the world of Google Apps, the adults have been coaching while the students, using Google docs, have made a Google Site dealing with their disaster, used the Google Spreadsheet to look across projects to draw major preparedness conclusions, used the calendar to schedule their activities, and, along with any other tool in Apps that might help them, researched, built, refined, analyzed, and synthesized their investigation. They first became experts in a single disaster and then developed the collaborative knowledge of dealing with any disaster.

The technological environment of Google Apps becomes transparent as the engagement of the problem at hand turns the class into group investigators. The concentration goes from trying to learn tools to building, thinking, solving, and sharing.

Such a reinvention of teaching and learning is a natural in the environment of Google Apps. The various tools are collaborative in nature by their very construction. They presume that collaborative environment rather than have to be tweaked to achieve it. This is very different than many content management systems costing thousands and thousands of dollars per year. Most often, those systems presume the older prescriptive teaching environment. Google Apps liberates both teacher and student from those restrictions.

Pushing It Yet Another Notch: Use a Knowledge Building Center

Google Apps allows us the opportunity to put higher level learning experiences into practice in a unique collaborative environment. We no longer think in terms of the isolated classroom. No longer need a sole teacher be responsible for the success of every single individual learner. Using Google Apps, the weight and frustration, including the intense stress, can be shouldered by a group of adults. We call these collaborative spaces Knowledge Building Centers and place them at the heart of the entire Google Apps for Education idea.

Knowledge Building centers can be the center of totally online learning or they can be the organizational element of face to face teaching or a combination of both online and physical space.

Using Google Sites or a variety of other tools, a simple "room" is created for each learning experience across the year. A sample Center template is shown below:

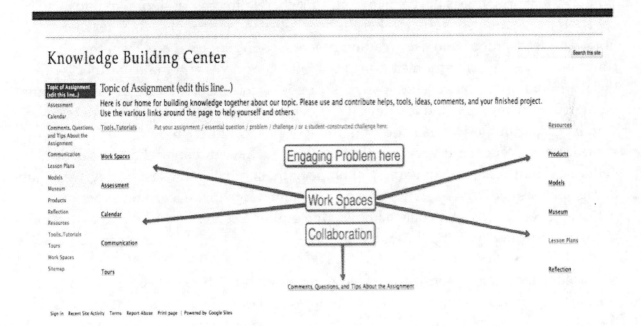

Instead of the classroom teacher being alone and creating isolated assignments, adults, specialists, classroom teachers, administrators, experts, and parents are building knowledge and learning how to learn skills together.

While this simple environment could be built using a variety of tools, notice the features of this template:

1. The hook or problem of the knowledge building environment is placed at the center and entices the learner to become engaged in the problem, question, or quest to be explored.
2. Around the central hook are various rooms where the adults and learners will do their work, building, and collaborating. There are rooms for tools, calendars to keep us on track, resources we all recommend, places to store our

21

products, a museum of previous projects, our assessments, the project plans, and, most important of all, a place where all the adults and the students are collaborating, helping, constructing, thinking, and communicating.

3. The knowledge building center for the unit can incorporate any of the Google Apps and other Web 2.0 extensions that are valuable for that learning experience. For example, students can be doing collaborative writing in a Google document; can be creating a video with Google Video; can be using a chat, email, and/or the knowledge building site to communicate and discuss progress; can be creating a Google presentation; can be using outside tools such as Voki to create and comment on presentations; doing digital storytelling podcasts; or a hundred other possibilities.

What is transformative is the change from a teacher's directive assignment into a collaborative learning experience. For the specialists in the school such as teacher librarians, teacher technologists, reading coaches, counselors, experts from the community, parents, or administrators, they find themselves automatic partners with the classroom teacher as coaches, partners, builders, and cheerleaders, all concentrating on high quality teaching and learning. The era of the isolated classroom teacher is over. And if both adults and learners do a big think or metacognitive reflection at the end of the learning experience, everyone reflects on how well we did and what we can do better next time. Like watching the videotape of the football game last Friday, we all are doing analysis and synthesis and looking for strategies to make learning experiences better and better across time. Each knowledge building center is one step in better and more sophisticated learning through technology.

Knowledge building centers can be the organizational structure to keep a face to face learning experience going. It can also be used as a space to work with other classes in the school, across schools, or across the world on a project together.

While students and adults might be somewhat wary the first few times they experience a collaborative knowledge building center as they figure out the collaborative nature of the space, they are very likely to take ownership of that work space and experience what we would term the construction of collective intelligence.

The Knowledge Building Center allows both adults and students to centralize everything needed to accomplish the central task before us. We can use a variety of tools within the Google family and beyond to help every learner grasp a deep understanding of the topic at hand. It is a perfect place for differentiation and teaching tool skills just in time as they are needed. The combination of skill and subject matter is likely to push both knowledge and the building of knowledge farther than if content teaching and skills teacher were separated as pictured below:

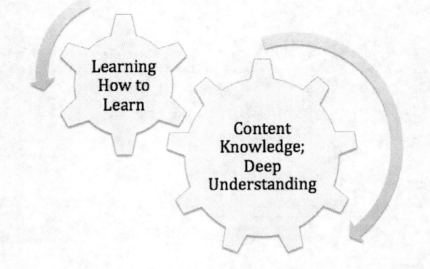

What we are saying is that adopting Google Apps for Education is not simply adopting a new technology for a school, it is the adoption of an entirely different philosophy of education away from the traditions of the 19th and 20th century models.

In the U.S. National Technology plan, this new vision is clearly outlined:

What 21st Century Learning Should Look Like

Figure 1 depicts a model of 21st century learning powered by technology. In contrast to traditional classroom instruction, which often consists of a single educator transmitting the same information to all learners in the same way, the model puts students at the center and empowers them to take control of their own learning by providing flexibility on several dimensions. A core set of standards-based concepts and competencies form the basis of what all students should learn, but beyond that students and educators have options for engaging in learning: large groups, small groups, and work tailored to individual goals, needs, and interests. (p. 10-11)

Figure 1. A Model of Learning

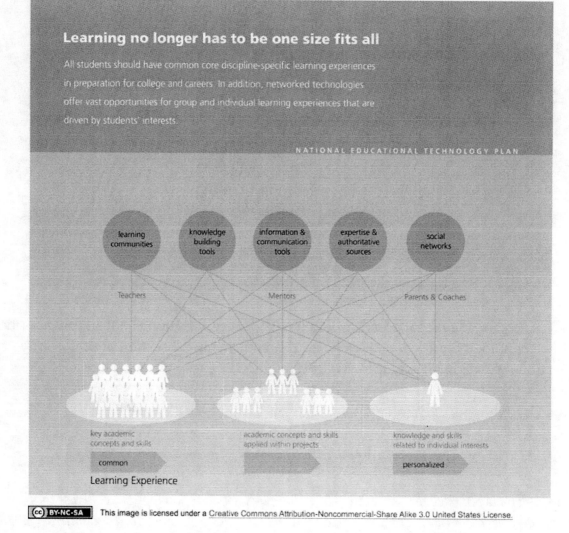

Achieving Results

Carol Koechlin and David Loertscher have been developing various visuals that demonstrate the kind of results to be expected in knowledge building centers. The following are some do's and don'ts.

Don't #1: Don't just concentrate on building content knowledge.

WHEN LEARNING HOW TO LEARN OR 21ST CENTURY SKILL PREDOMINATE

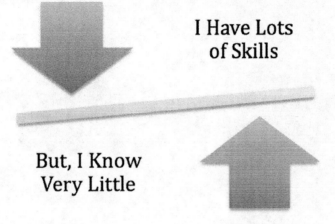

I Have Lots of Skills

But, I Know Very Little

Don't #2: Don't just teach 21st Century Skills.

WHEN CONTENT KNOWLEDGE PREDOMINATES

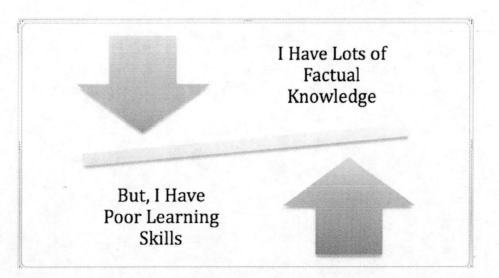

I Have Lots of Factual Knowledge

But, I Have Poor Learning Skills

Do #1: Bring a balance between content and learning to learn into a learning experience.

WHAT ABOUT A BALANCE OF THE TWO?

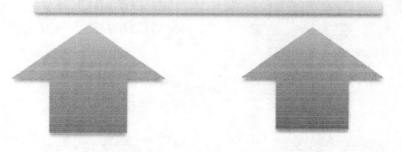

I Know How to Learn

And, I am Knowlegeable

Do#2: Make the Knowledge Building Center truly collaborative.

COLLABORATION RUBRIC

Isolation:	Cooperation:	Collaboration:
Separation of classroom and learning commons	Coordinated teaching but at different times and locations	Beginning to end co-teaching and assessment

Do #3: Design the Knowledge Building Center in such a way that collaboration is a natural.

KBC COLLABORATIVE ENVIRONMENT

One-way: Traditional teacher designed assignment

Two-way: Sharing in design and learning

All-way: Everyone working, building, creating

Do #4: Use a quality instructional design as the plan within the knowledge building center.

INSTRUCTIONAL DESIGN USED

Traditional: research, present, assess

Constructivist: higher-level questions, content + process, inventive sharing

Transformative personal expertise and collaborative intelligence; content + process; Big Think

Do #5: Create realistic assessments that measure a more complete picture of what was learned.

ASSESSMENT DESIGN USED

| Assessment of Learning: Summative | Assessment for Learning: Formative, feedback, coaching, summative | Assessment as Learning: Formative, feedback, coaching, summative for both teachers and students |

Do #6: Select technologies used to boost learning.

TECHNOLOGY BOOST TO TEACHING AND LEARNING

| Techno-Traditional: Simple transfer to technology | Engaging: Using techno-fascination | Transformative: Inventive push by technology that boosts learning and skills |

Do #7: Draw upon the strengths of what the learners already know and the skills they have.

KNOWLEDGE BUILDING WORLDS

Do #8: Draw upon student's strengths in systematic ways.

KNOWLEDGE BUILDING WORLDS

Accidental:
Unplanned / appeals to some learners

Planned:
Some integration of skills / higher rate of success

Sustained:
Engagement of learners and co-teaching of skills by learners

By taking these principles into account during the design, the activities, the assessment, and the concluding big think, the likelihood of a remarkable lean ring experience that engages every learner is exponentially better.

Resources

Loertscher, David V., Carol Koechlin, and Sandi Zwaan. *Beyond Bird Units: Thinking and Understanding in Information-Rich and Technology-Rich Environments*. Available from Amazon.com or from LMCSource.com

National Educational Technology Plan, 2010. *Transforming American Education: Learning Powered by Technology*. At: http://www.ed.gov/technology/netp-2010

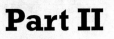

Part II

The Tools as Knowledge Building Enablers

Chapter 6

Google Apps Education Edition: An Overview

Google Apps Education Edition is a suite of tools within a safe and free environment you set up for your school. Your school, school district, or even your state department of education can apply for membership. For example, the state of Oregon has set up a contract for the entire state's schools. If your school is not already a member, you apply for membership and you need to set up a web domain name for your school. All work within your domain resides in the cloud; i.e., it does not reside on the school's local servers. Thus, the entire system is available to any of the students or adults from any computer that has access to the Internet and at any time or from any location.

Google keeps making changes and improvements to its suite of tools available to member schools but at this writing, the tools consisted of:

- **Gmail**—internal email within your school; not the outside email for the whole world.
- **Google Calendar**—for personal organization, group schedules, class schedules/assignments, and even whole school events.
- **Google Docs**—a suite of tools consisting of:
  - **Documents**—a collaborative word processor.
  - **Spreadsheets**—a collaborative spreadsheet good for number crunching and collaborative idea collection in real time.
  - **Forms**—a survey or questionnaire tool that populates a spreadsheet like Survey Monkey. Forms can be used not only for surveys but also for quizzes that score themselves.
  - **Presentations**—presentation software like PowerPoint but not as complex.
- **Google Video**—akin to your own internal YouTube.
- **Google Sites**—Web page construction tool that can be used either as a web site or a wiki.
- **Google Start page**—a personalized home page for every user, whether student or adult.
- **Google Mobile**—a service that helps anyone access Google Apps via a variety of personal digital devices such as Blackberrys, iPads, and cell phones.
- **Administrative tools**—gives power to a school or district administrator to open or close any of the above tools to users and tools to manage security.

As this book goes to press, a host of other tools have been added to the list above. These will be covered in Appendix A.

Of all the tools that are available and those that will be added as this suite continues to evolve, we recommend you begin with the basic documents, spreadsheets, and presentations. One good way to get started is for the teacher to become somewhat familiar with the tool first, then have a small group of students in the class introduced to the tool to "play with" before the entire class launches its learning experience. The geek squad with the teacher can do a quick dry run in a planning session and things are likely to go much better during the opening working session with a large group. The attitude becomes one of "you teach me; I teach you; and we all learn the tool together." As the tool itself becomes transparent, then the emphasis is completely on the learning. As the class takes advantage of the tool's efficiencies, they are able to accomplish more learning in less time in addition to learning a new tool skill.

In the following chapters, we cover each tool in the suite with accompanying ideas for knowledge building. All the knowledge building ideas are indexed at the end of the book so that you can look up terms such as "collaborative writing" to find our recommendation for a tool to use matched to a Common Core Standard or 21st Century Skill.

Selected Resources and Bibliography

- In an attempt to keep up with changes at Google, try their **Google New** service at: http://www.google.com/newproducts/

- Excellent video introducing Google Apps at: http://www.google.com/educators/p_docs.html

- Slides from the Google Teacher Academy listing advantages of using Google Apps: http://sites.google.com/site/gtaresources/2008-11-18/docs

- A helpful guide to Google Docs used in the Google Teacher Academy program (PDF file): http://sites.google.com/site/gtaresources/files/Crib_Docs.pdf?attredirects=0

- Richard Byrne does a good job in keeping up with Google and a number of other Web 2.0 tools in his Free Technology for Teachers blog at: http://www.freetech4teachers.com

- Google now has a YouTube collaborative community about Google Docs at: http://www.youtube.com/GoogleDocsCommunity

Chapter 7

Google Documents

Introduction

The Document Tool in Google Apps for Education is a simple and straightforward word processor with the innovative feature of simultaneous collaborative writing on the same document. If teachers begin with this tool, often familiar to students, they can find immediate uses that start everyone off on a paperless and sharing journey.

Description

A Google Document is similar to any other basic word processor, but differs because more than one person can be editing the same document simultaneously. The document is stored in the cloud and can be accessed only by its author or others as the author chooses. Thus, the document is available from any computer linked to the Internet.

For adults, it is a familiar although limited word processing environment. As the authors of this book, we are using Docs to construct this entire book. This is because once a particular document is shared, the sharers can work on the document simultaneously. The familiar tool bar at the top of the page helps students do enough formatting for most unsophisticated writing projects. Another valuable feature is auto saving. Almost as soon as a word or sentence is created, it is saved in the cloud for access anytime and anywhere.

Getting Started

For those with an email address, the word Documents is at the top of the email screen at all times. Users with other email can merely type Google Docs into their search engine and bring up the documents tab. Google will want the user to have a legitimate email address to use the documents, spreadsheets, forms, and presentations software.

To get started, first, find the Documents link:

Then select Document:

Begin typing, using the tool bar to format the work, save the document under a name you choose, and then share the document with those you wish:

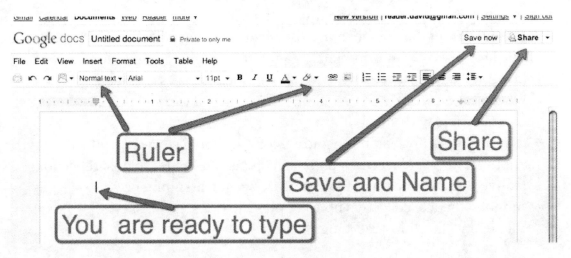

After you have named and shared the document, those who have access can now simultaneously edit the document. We suggest having the various collaborators choose a color so that everyone knows who is making revisions. If more than one person is editing the document at the same time, there will be a visible cursor for each person and you will all see words appear in real time. While upwards of 50 people can simultaneously edit the document, multiple writers require more and more bandwidth.

Advantages

Google Docs contains the same advantages that any word processing has, including the efficiencies of writing, editing, and formatting text. In addition, since the actual document is stored "in the cloud," it can be accessed on any computer hooked to the Internet. This saves server space needs at the school and the need for easy-to-us thumb drives to transport documents. And because it is collaborative in nature, the document can be shared with a teacher or other partners for viewing or editing. Thus, the need for printing is reduced.

The biggest advantage of using shared Google Documents is the ability for the teacher to easily see and comment on students' writing. If a teachers asks students to write a long essay, the teacher can critique the essay and give constructive suggestions before the students "hand in" the essay. Also, the essay can be saved into the student's electronic portfolio and use as a resource by future teachers to see strengths and weaknesses in a student's literacy skills. If the teacher or fellow students would like to make a comment rather than actually edit the document, one can "insert" a comment from the tool bar.

Sample Uses

- Teachers can employ Google Docs to practice keyboarding and initial use of machine writing assists such as spell checkers, simple formatting, and the placement of pictures or other illustrations in text.
- Live links from the document can be made to notes, websites used, sources that have been used for information, or quotations making it easy for the reader to check original sources used.
- Writing can be translated in and out of various languages and used for work across borders with collaborating groups.
- All types of writing can be encouraged from digital storytelling to journeying to serious writing and research papers, responses to issues, plans, reflections, creative writing, and any other genre or written assignment.
- Students can take collective notes of presentations, guest speakers, videos, or other events they are observing.

- Students create and edit their own help guides which are shared with the entire class. For example, students in a grade 11 math class created "help guides" to help themselves and others with Google App spreadsheet assignments. These help guides are now available for the next group of grade 11 students.

Learning with Google Docs

With the increased emphasis in many schools on quality writing, the opportunity to have a tool that can be used to promote individuals and collaborative writing is the innovative part of this tool. It is not just the mechanics of pulling ideas from a variety of sources into a coherent summary or synthesis, it is the quality of the presentation that exhibits deep understanding of the topic at hand and a carefully laid out argument and logical progression of ideas that can be constructed alone or in groups.

For the formal research report or paper, the collaborative environment makes writing, revising, and polishing possible with relative ease. Fellow students or teachers can add comments to the document for correction, missing elements, assessment, suggestion, or congratulation as pictured below:

Quote from s student response paper:

I like the uropean version on cinder ella better than the other ones becuz it is like the Disney movie.

Sam: you need to compare the European version of Cinderella with one of the others from Asia or Africa your heard. Also, please correct your spelling - reader.david

In checking various writing standards to be achieved, compare those standards with the tools available in Google Docs. Build and share ideas for using the tool across types informational text creating and creative writing. Utilize the sharing and annotating functions to build the kind of writing skills that push novice writers into experienced, creative, and critical writers.

Notice the role that the Google Document tool can have in building writes as envisioned by the U.S. Common Core Anchor Standards for writing K–12:

Text Types and Purposes

1. *Write arguments to support claims in an analysis of substantive topics or texts, using valid reasoning and relevant and sufficient evidence.*
2. *Write informative/explanatory texts to examine and convey complex ideas and information clearly and accurately through the effective selection, organization, and analysis of content.*
3. *Write narratives to develop real or imagined experiences or events using effective technique, well-chosen details, and well-structured event sequences.*

Production and Distribution of Writing

4. *Produce clear and coherent writing in which the development, organization, and style are appropriate to task, purpose, and audience.*
5. *Develop and strengthen writing as needed by planning, revising, editing, rewriting, or trying a new approach.*
6. *Use technology, including the Internet, to produce and publish writing and to interact and collaborate with others.*

Research to Build and Present Knowledge

7. *Conduct short as well as more sustained research projects based on focused questions, demonstrating understanding of the subject under investigation.*
8. *Gather relevant information from multiple print and digital sources, assess the credibility and accuracy of each source, and integrate the information while avoiding plagiarism.*
9. *Draw evidence from literary or informational texts to support analysis, reflection, and research.*

Range of Writing

10. *Write routinely over extended time frames (time for research, reflection, and revision) and shorter time frames (a single sitting or a day or two) for a range of tasks, purposes, and audiences.*

Notice that these standards emphasize both the development of personal and collaborative writing skills and the use of technologies to produce products. Google Documents is a fabulous tool to accomplish these goals.

Issues

Over the last several years, there have been a number of major improvements made to the functionality and sophistication level of Google Documents. There is no reason to believe that this will not continue. In the meantime, other tools will need to be used for more sophisticated formatting and publishing needs that students will require.

Chapter 8

Google Spreadsheets

Introduction

We might think that the typical spreadsheet would be a favorite of math, science, and business teachers, but the Google spreadsheet has unique features that make it a favorite tool across all disciplines. Yes, the spreadsheet can crunch numbers very well, but we can think of it as an organizational place to store and manipulate facts and ideas. If we use the spreadsheet for numbers, then formulas are used to do analysis, computation, and representation of the data. For facts and ideas, the analysis, synthesis, and conclusions will depend totally on a student's higher order thinking.

Description

The spreadsheet has been around since the early days of computing. However, the collaborative nature of a spreadsheet has only been available on very sophisticated tools until Google added the collaborative feature to its simple tool. There is a limit of 50 simultaneous collaborators. We understand that the composition of a spreadsheet is a series of cells in rows and columns which can be used for numbers or text. If used for numbers, formulas can be added to columns or rows to do calculations and to create graphical representations of the data such as bar or pie charts.

Spreadsheets can also be linked to online forms which allows students to create their own surveys that automatically graph the results in real time. School administrators could use these forms to quickly survey students. For example, we might use the on-line forms to survey students on their experiences with cyber-bullying. See more ideas about creating forms in the following chapter.

For more advanced users, spreadsheets also support the use of Java Scripting, which allows users to create a wide array of applications such as the ability to automatically generate and send personalized emails directly from the spreadsheet with data inputted on a form.

Getting Started

Creating a spreadsheet is relatively simple. We suggest watching a few tutorials first, reading our ideas and then creating your own.

First, go to the Google Documents tab; find and click on the CREATE NEW tab and select "spreadsheet."

Second, create your columns and rows as you want the students to see it, save and name it, and then share it with your students as shown below.

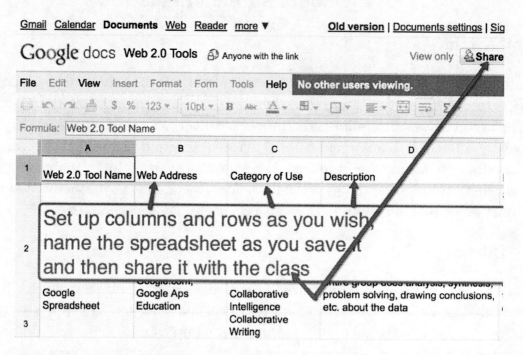

Third, the entire class can be working on this one sheet simultaneously. If a student is editing a particular cell, a box appears instantly on everyone's screen and they must select another cell to be working in as shown below.

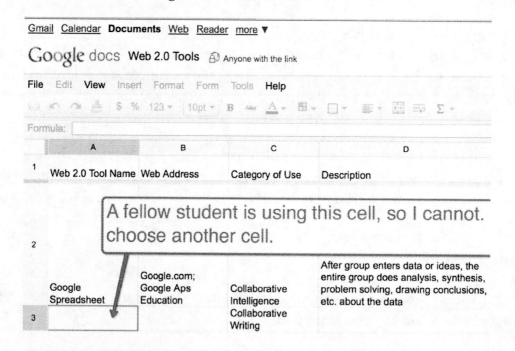

If using the spreadsheet for numbers, calculations, and charts or graphs, watch several tutorials in order to create formulas and use the data to create the various charts available.

Advantages

- The students can enter numbers, words, or fairly short ideas into the cells simultaneously.
- The teacher and the students can watch the spreadsheet populate in real time. If groups or individuals are having trouble, it is easy to give advice.
- The teacher can control who can edit the spreadsheet.
- The spreadsheet can contain gadgets, illustrations, and graphs. Check Google tutorials for directions.

Sample Uses

- Students could enter numbers, dollar amounts, or measurements from their experiments or from data sources they are probing. When everyone has entered their share of the data needed, the spreadsheet can calculate and draw appropriate graphs for analysis and synthesis by the class as a whole. Many hands have made light work.
- Individuals or groups of students are assigned various facts to collect and enter them into the appropriate columns and rows on the spreadsheet as they are able to find the needed fact. Example: the names of languages spoken in various countries; the favorite flavors of ice cream by each class member; the name of states that have laws for or against gay marriage.
- Individuals or groups of students record brief sentences or phrases (too much text in a cell makes the entire sheet difficult to analyze). Examples: Brief arguments about various issues in columns that are for or against; major ideas listed from complex texts or a variety of texts; individual student responses to an idea or problem. When all the ideas have been entered, individuals or small groups can synthesize ideas down and/or across the columns to sift out the major big ideas or conclusions from what has been entered.
- Survey any group of math teachers and ask them "What is the single best software application to teach numeracy skills?" They are likely agree on spreadsheets because they allow students to create and play with different mathematical scenarios and get immediate feedback, including charts and graphs, which is great for the visual learner. Spreadsheets allow students to work more efficiently and help them organize and share their work. Online spreadsheets are also designed to easily gather online data and statistics and allow students to do real life applications such as gathering statistics from different countries and generating different types of statistical reports and

graphs. Also all spreadsheets can either be viewed as a web page or embedded into the student's virtual space.

- The spreadsheet can also be used for organizational functions by either the teachers or the students. Here is an example of a calendared scheduling of a shared space such as the library, computer lab, or learning commons:

| File | Edit | View | Insert | Format | Form | Tools | Help |

Formula:

	A	B	C	D	E	F	G	H	I	J
1										
2		January 2009							January Schedule	
3	Su	M	Tu	W	Th	F	Sa			
4					1	2	3			
5	4	5	6	7	8	9	10			
6	11	12	13	14	15	16	17			
7	18	19	20	21	22	23	24			
8	25	26	27	28	29	30	31			
9										
10		February 2009							February Schedule	
11	Su	M	Tu	W	Th	F	Sa			
12	1	2	3	4	5	6	7			
13	8	9	10	11	12	13	14			
14	15	16	17	18	19	20	21			
15	22	23	24	25	26	27	28			
16										
17										
18		March 2009							March Schedule	
19	Su	M	Tu	W	Th	F	Sa			

Learning with Google Spreadsheets

- **Analysis and Synthesis** are higher order thinking skills that are often in limited supply in traditional education. When students do the finding, locating, copying, and pasting of data or ideas into the spreadsheet, the basic work has been accomplished. Certainly this first phase can be used to teach principles of quality data. Quality data must be found, discovered, and measured if phase two is going to succeed. If there is bad data in the cells, conclusions will be faulty. So, after everyone has "certified" that the best data and ideas have been entered, the next round raises the ante. As individuals or small groups, have students analyze what has been entered. They can look for patterns and trends, compute numbers, compute results, and do critical thinking about what the data mean. Perhaps there are varying perspectives of what is there; perhaps there are clear-cut conclusions; perhaps there are more questions and answers. Use the cells below or beside the original data sets for the analysis and synthesis to appear. Perhaps different groups will see differing conclusions than can be re-analyzed and rethought. What are the overarching ideas, meanings, and results of the investigation?

- **Collaborative Work.** Using a spreadsheet to advantage presumes that everyone is contributing quality information to the collective work. This provides a great opportunity to teach the collaborative work ethics: "I/we are responsible to get the work done on time and with high quality standards."

- **Higher Order Thinking.** In individual or collaborative assignments, teachers often suspect that students have plagiarized what they submit without real understanding of the topic at hand. By using a spreadsheet, students are entering the best data they can find and this can be cited if needed or not. However, in phase two, plagiarism is not an issue since students must find meaning out of the data that has been entered. Critical thinking and creative thinking come to the top instantly.

- **Examples of real analysis and synthesis:**
  - Students worked with the Forest Service collected temperature data from a variety of mountain streams in the local area. Experts came to the class and looked across all the spreadsheet data and worked with individuals, classes, and across participating schools to draw conclusions and brainstorm possible action steps.
  - In a local election of contentious issues, students interviewed a variety of citizens about their opinions and entered summaries of positions in the spreadsheet. Before the election was held, the students looked at the strength of the various arguments in an attempt to predict the outcome. After the election, the students interviewed opinion leaders to analyze how their predictions had failed or succeeded.
  - In doing a character analysis of actors in a classical drama, students entered their perceptions of character traits into the spreadsheet. In the analysis phase, students discovered that they did not all agree and used the data to try to arrive at a consensus about the characters. Then they compared their synthesis with those of prominent literary critics for further discussion.
  - Country by country, students tried to locate the best statistics about the percentage of the population that were infected with AIDS. They compared these statistics to local, state, regional, or national statistics of their own area. Then they ask "So what?" and "What's next?"
  - Younger students compared the calorie counts of the number 1 meal at a variety of local fast food restaurants. They searched databases, books, and

local experts to compare their findings and the implications for their personal buying habits.

- Learning need not be reserved for students. In a professional development session where teachers are studying a document such as the U.S. Common Core Standards, instead of a lecture that no one will be likely to remember, the principal set up a spreadsheet. Teachers were put in groups to first extract from the document major ideas as pictured below:

Reading	Writing
Major Points Affecting TLs	**Major Points Affecting TLs**
Literature	

This allowed all the teachers to actively participate in understanding various pieces and parts of the document. After this activity, the teachers were jigsawed and they began looking both down the various columns and across the various columns to make recommendations for actual progress in what they do (in our example, they were looking at what the library/learning commons program could do for the entire faculty):

Reading	Writing
Implications for Library/Learning Commons Programs	**Implications for Library/Learning Commons Programs**

The assumption of the principal was that while the exercise would take a bit more time than a quick lecture by PowerPoint, the difference for school improvement would be substantial.

Selected Resources

- Official Google Spreadsheet tutorial: http://docs.google.com/support/bin/static.py?hl=en&page=guide.cs&guide=20322

- Google Help Site: http://docs.google.com/support/bin/topic.py?hl=en&topic=15115

- A 2009 tutorial for beginners: http://www.youtube.com/watch?v=G-AnN51Xco8

- Official Google training tutorial http://edutraining.googleapps.com/Training-Home/module-4-docs/chapter-4

- Google spreadsheet scripting tutorial http://code.google.com/googleapps/appsscript/guide.html

- A 2009 tutorial in Spanish: http://vimeo.com/4110793

Chapter 9

Google Forms

Introduction

Google Forms is a survey tool similar to the popular Survey Monkey. The creator builds a question bank that can be answered as a paragraph, multiple choice, rating, or brief answer survey or quiz. Every person who fills in the form unwittingly populates a spreadsheet for instant analysis by the teacher. While surveys are very useful, the form can also be used as part of a research project where students collect various information to feed into the solution of a problem or an essential question that a class is confronting. Alternately, it can be used as the first step in the use of the Google Spreadsheet for knowledge building.

Description

Think of Google Forms as a questionnaire or survey that can be answered by a few or by many participants. Questions can be created and the answers can be in the form of multiple choice, rating scales, short answer, or longer answer responses. Any questions can be labeled as required or can just be optional. For example, if the creator requires the respondent's name, one can track not only who answered but also the resulting spreadsheet will time and date stamp that response. When the respondent finishes answering the questions and clicks the SUBMIT button, that response will automatically be added to a spreadsheet where all respondent's data is presented and ready for analysis. The creator of the form is given a URL for the form that can be sent out to potential respondents and also a URL for the resultant spreadsheet.

Getting Started

Most of the tutorials we have watched begin by constructing the form or questionnaire as a first step. We prefer to begin by setting up the resulting spreadsheet first, since that is where the actual analysis and synthesis will take place. We recommend that you watch a variety of video tutorials before you begin (a few are listed in selected resources), and you can also follow our steps here:

First: Create a new spreadsheet and plan the columns for each question you will ask the student:

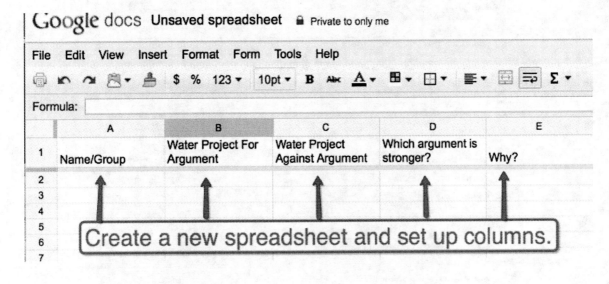

Second: Save and name the spreadsheet, then click on Form:

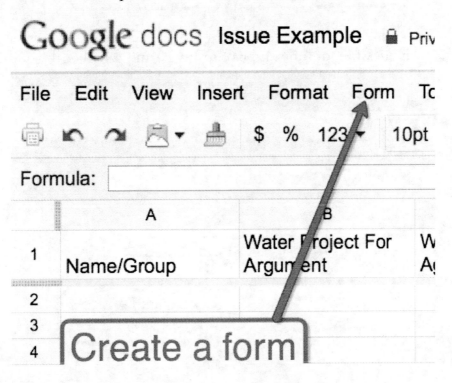

Third: All of your questions will appear automatically in the form. Hover over each part of the questionnaire to edit what you want:

Fourth: Edit each question for hints, type of response and whether the question is to be required:

Fifth: Choose a theme:

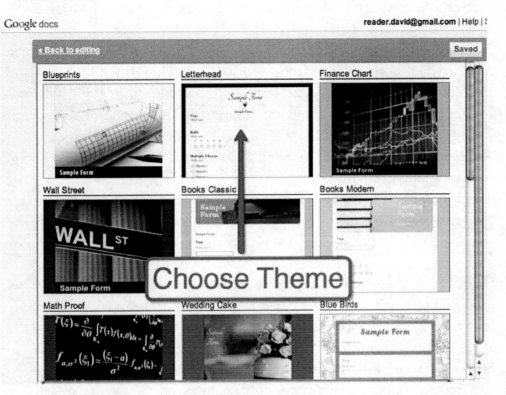

Sixth: When the student clicks on the URL supplied, this is the completed questionnaire. Congratulations!

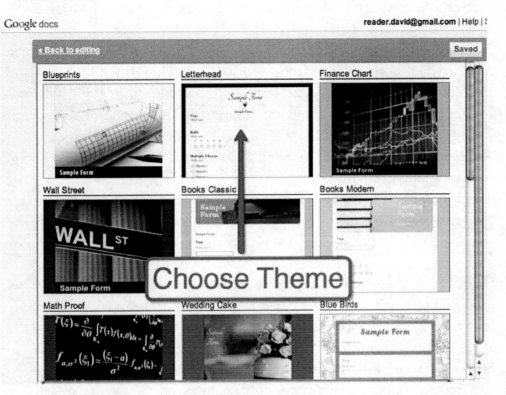

Advantages

- Instead of a huge grid of a spreadsheet, students see an uncluttered questionnaire where they can complete their responses.
- By requiring a name, the teacher can watch the spreadsheet populate in real time and can ascertain if a group or individual is having difficulty. (Yes, students can misidentify themselves and they can fill in the questions multiple times...)
- Students can do their research and fill out the questionnaire during class or a library period or they can do their questionnaires as homework.
- As long as the students or respondents have the URL, they can respond to the questionnaire from any computer connected to the Internet.
- The resulting spreadsheet time stamps each submission so that you know when the form was completed.

Sample Uses

- Students of all ages can survey one another, parents, community, or other schools anywhere in the world on a wide variety of topics for patterns, ideas, to compare and contrast, or just informal information.
- A teacher can create quick quizzes to be answered in or outside class.
- Students can research data including numbers, facts, or ideas and record their findings in the questionnaire without seeing what others are entering at the moment.
- Students can take or create polls that measure attitudes about a situation or problem for instant analysis.
- A survey can serve as a progress report by individuals or groups on a major project.
- Teachers, administrators, or specialists such as a teacher technologist or reading coach can query the faculty about issues confronting the group.
- Real math problems can be created where various data and data analyses are tried by the students both as a math application but also to make sense of the meaning generated by various formulas.
- Forms can also be used to create online quizzes and tests. Students can be required to log-in so that their name is automatically recorded. Also if the quiz or test is multiple choice it can a be setup so it automatically marks itself. Below is practice literacy test to help students in Ontario prepare for the grade 10 standardized literary test.

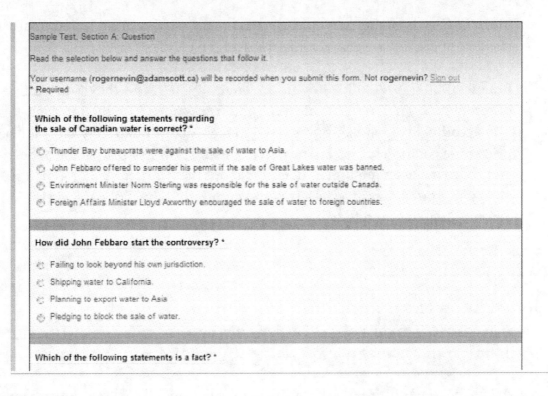

- Mark Wagner created a blog post where he illustrates the use of Goolge Forms to create self-graded quizzes at: http://edtechlife.com/?p=2600

Learning with Google Spreadsheets

- **Formative Assessment.** As a part of a multiple-day research project in the library, Doug Achterman, Teacher Librarian at San Benito High School in Hollister, CA, has students fill out a two or three question form as the last thing they do at the end of each research period. Doug and the teacher use this information to know student progress, who is in trouble, and what they need to do during the next day's research period to push progress toward completion. As coaches, they use this as an informal formative assessment.

- **Analysis and Synthesis.** As illustrated above in our getting started segment, a class has been assigned to research either as groups or individuals an argument both for and against a community water project that is coming up for vote by the City Council. They use the form to record the arguments they consider significant, make some judgments, and finally, but looking at the spreadsheet, can summarize their research in order to plan a presentation to the City Council.

- **Compare and Contrast.** Students are comparing the story of Cinderella as it appears across many cultures. A google form is created with a question about each character in the version they are reading: "Describe the character Cinderella in your version." After the spreadsheet is populated, the students are jigsawed into groups where they compare one character across cultures, and finally the class compares all the characters across all the cultures.

- **Financial Literacy:** Math students are entering the prices they find for five different items in various local stores and from sources on the Internet. Taking into account, taxes and shipping, they make a determination what is the best price for a comparable item. They compute the range of prices, the average price, and try to make an intelligent decision about their purchase. For a mad free for all, try this on planning a class trip and computing the costs of travel, accommodations, and food.

___

Selected Resources
- A good 2009 introduction to Google Forms by a classroom teacher: http://www.youtube.com/watch?v=GFYu4r0q25k

- A 2009 beginner tutorial on creating a form but does not show the accompanying spreadsheet: http://www.screentoaster.com/watch/stVU5WQEJIR11ZQ1VdWltcU1VT/google_forms_instructions

- A 2009 tutorial that begins with building your spreadsheet first and then the accompanying form: http://www.youtube.com/watch?v=YxYZKkusg-Y

- A 2009 Forms tutorial that concentrates on an opinion survey: http://vimeo.com/6028391

- A useful 2009 Tutorial about embedding a Google Form into a blog: http://www.viddler.com/explore/bneiswender/videos/20/

Chapter 10

Google Docs: Presentations

Introduction:

Presentations can be considered a simple and unsophisticated "PowerPoint" presentation tool. Alongside Documents, this is probably the most familiar software to students who are and have been subjected to death by PowerPoint. In this brief overview, we concentrate on effective ways to use Presentations as learning tools rather and regurgitation exercises.

Description

Creators of presentations can select from a variety of templates to use in formatting slide messages together with various theme backgrounds. Pictures and videos can be embedded in the slides but not audio at the time of writing, although the latter is a very much requested feature. Below each slide, creators can add speaker notes that can be useful to the presenter but also to teachers who are assessing the content of the presentation as a whole. Like other Google Docs tools, Presentations can be shared with others and thus can be collaboratively edited and created.

Getting Started

Getting started with a presentation is simple and a quick demonstration and relying on knowledgeable students will spread the expertise easily among a class. First, create a new presentation:

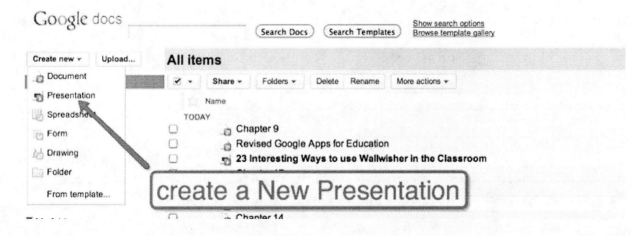

Next, select any formatting needed:

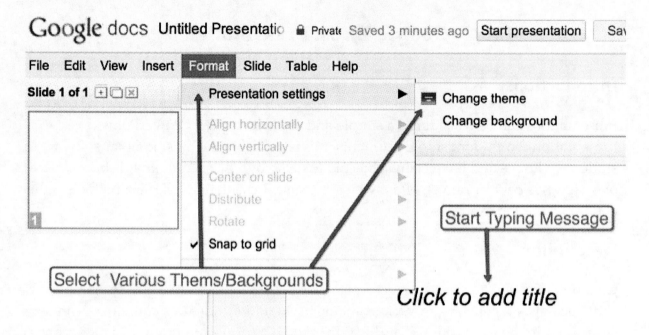

Pay attention to the Insert tab:

Save and name the presentation; then, share it with others. Share early if you wish to have others collaborate in the construction of the presentation. If you wish to have speaker notes, check in the lower right hand corner of the screen:

Click to add title

Click to add subtitle

Click in the lower right to add speaker notes → ⌇+

Check out other online tutorials of Google Presentations to discover other features.

Advantages

- Presentations is free and available from any computer connected to the Internet. This promotes equity both in and out of school, across schools, and across the world.
- Presentations is very simple to learn and use.
- Collaborative building of a presentation is possible through sharing whether this is among friends, different classes, across schools, or across the world.

Sample Uses

- The usual reason why presentations are so ubiquitous across schools is the idea that if one understands an idea and is able to present it, deep understanding occurs.
- The assumption is made that the audience will learn the content of the presentation from the presenter.
- Use Presentations for students to create quick tutorials. For example, the getting started visuals above were created with Google Presentations and Jing, an outside free tool that can do screen shots and short videos of what is happening on the screen.
- Have students create one or two-slide presentations that illustrate difficult concepts of the topic at hand. Have a kind of competition between slides that are illustrating the same concept. Have students pick the ones that help them understand the best.

- Have a group or the entire class create and present ideas to administrators, parents, government groups, school boards, etc.
- Have students create presentations in other languages being learned or to communicate across the world.

Learning with Google Presentations

It is not uncommon to have students use a technology such as presentations that are designed to build and exhibit deep understanding and have the effort fail. Poor construction and presentation techniques can mislead as much as illuminate. The time it takes to present one presentation after another to a bored audience can be counter productive.

- **Glitz vs. Content**. Students often mistake cool presentation features, images, and an inclusion of videos as a substitute for sound content. Teachers should build assessment rubrics that prize content over technique. If a particular technique enhances understanding by the viewer, all the better.
- **Digital Citizenship.** Hurried presentations with tight deadlines often contain plagiarized material and images without citation. Ask the teacher librarian to work alongside both students and teachers to teach the ideas of copyright and fair use. Where can copyright-free images be located? How can we quote and cite materials used? Required presentation notes can be useful for citing appropriate sources and students can learn how to cite images from a bank such as the Creative Commons. The best way to avoid plagiarism is to ask students better questions. For example, if a comparison must be made, the student can copy two ideas but has to be able to understand the ideas to make the comparison. If plagiarism is a common problem, it is an adult problem, not a student problem. Better and higher level questions are the key that usually makes plagiarism a non-issue.
- **Individual and collaborative expertise**. Reward outstanding presentations that exhibit either or both individual understanding or group creativity that exhibit collective understanding. It is all about what I know and understand and what we know and understand. For example, individual presentations focusing on one culture can be used as the basis for a new presentation that looks at cross cultural comparisons. Presentations about bad science experiments can be combined to exhibit the way to judge the difference between bad science and good science. Presentations designed to convince can be compared to discover principles of good argument, advertising and the recognition of spin and propaganda techniques.
- **Teach the skill of quality presentations**. Is reading the content of slides one after one a great audience grabbing technique? What is the balance between text on

the screen and what is being said orally? How well do visuals support the written message? How does the presenter engage the audience in an activity rather than a passive march through the forest of boredom? How much can the ear stand before any distraction is prayed for?

- **Vary Presentations.** Just because a presentation has been prepared is no reason that the entire class has to watch it! The teacher may be the only viewer, a small group may watch and critique it, a teacher librarian might examine the presentation to assess information use. The traditional serial presentation by each student is a huge waste of time and listeners are as likely as not to tune the event out and text their friends under the table. If both presenter and/or audience are not actively engaged, plan a different use for presentations.

Selected Resources

- Seth Goodin's blog post about bad PowerPoints: http://sethgodin.typepad.com/seths_blog/2007/01/really_bad_powe.html

- David S. Rose on how to create a pitch via PowerPoint to venture capitalists. Good to teach students how to be convincing: http://www.ted.com/index.php/talks/david_s_rose_on_pitching_to_vcs.html

- An example of a powerful but brief presentation for high school students on what it takes to be a success: http://www.allaboutpresentations.com/2010/03/ted-talks-8-secrets-of-success-in-just.html

- Tips on making great presentations: http://www.brighthub.com/computing/windows-platform/articles/41661.aspx

Chapter 11

Google Calendar

Introduction

Google Calendar is an electronic calendar in many ways similar to Apple's iCal or a multitude of other electronic calendars currently available. The big difference between Google Calendar and most of these other calendars though is that Google Calendar can be shared in a collaborative manner with other users. Google Calendar also allows users to embed calendars into websites or publish calendars for others to see via a specified URL. Users can also choose to subscribe to Google Calendars provided the calendars in question have been made public.

Advantages

Google Calendar has several advantages over its more traditional brethren. First and foremost is its ability to be accessed by users from anywhere with access to the Internet (the cloud). More significantly, however, is its ability to be shared in a collaborative manner with other users or with the general public via a published URL or via a website the calendar is embedded in.

Sample Uses
- Teachers, school administrators and others can publish Google Calendars containing important assignments, dates, etc. for students and other stake holders to see and utilize.
- Students can create and share Google Calendars with their student project-partners and with their teachers to better plan progression goals.
- Google Calendars can even be synced with mobile devices to allow users to both view and, in some cases, change the content of shared calendars.

Getting Started

Google Calendar is included in the Google Apps for Education suite. To start using Google Calendar, users simply click on the "Calendar" link at the upper left-hand corner of their Google Apps for Education accounts and begin scheduling.

Users can also create multiple Google Calendars for their own use or for embedding, sharing and/or publishing. To create a new Google Calendar, users simply click the "Add" link under the "My Calendars" box to the middle left of their displayed Google Calendar and follow the directions therein. To embed, share or publish Google Calendars, users follow the "Settings" link in the "My Calendars" box, and choose the "Share This Calendar" link.

Once the "Settings" link has been followed, users can follow the "Share this calendar" link, then choose to share the selected Google Calendar to specified users via email addresses, share it with only a range of people, or they can they can choose to make the calendar visible to everyone by clicking the box next to "Make this calendar public."

Google Calendars can also be shared via URLs by going to the "Calendar Details" portion of the menu and choosing the "Calendar Address" link and following the resulting instructions. Users wishing to embed calendars into existing websites simply need to cut and paste the html code available to the right of the "Embed This Calendar" option in the same "Calendar Details" portion of the menu. Of course, these shared, published and/or embedded calendars can always be unshared, unpublished or un-embedded should the user choose to reduce other users' access.

Search my calendars Show search options

mr.m.melton@jlmslibraryapps.com Details

Calendar Details   Share this Calendar   Notifications

◄ Back to calendar (Save) (Cancel)

Calendar Name:	mr.m.melton@jlmslibraryapps.com
Calendar Owner:	"Micah Melton" <mr.m.melton@jlmslibraryapps.com>
Organization:	James Lick Middle School
Description:	

Use the code to embed the Calendar into a website.

Location: e.g. "San Francisco" or "New York" or "USA." Specifying a general location will help people find events on your calendar (if it's public)

Calendar Time Zone: This calendar uses your current time zone: (GMT-08:00) Pacific Time Set my time zone

Embed This Calendar
Embed this calendar in your website or blog by pasting this code into your web page. To embed multiple calendars, click on the Customize Link

Paste this code into your website.
Customize the color, size, and other options

```
<iframe
src="http://www.google.com/calendar/hosted/jlmslibrarya
pps.com/embed?
src=mr.m.melton%40jlmslibraryapps.com&ctz=America/
Los_Angeles" style="border: 0" width="800"
```

Calendar Address: XML ICAL HTML (mr.m.melton@jlmslibraryapps.com)

Share the Calendar via URL.

Learn more
Change sharing settings

This is the address for your calendar. No one can use this link unless you have made your calendar public.

◄ Back to calendar (Save) (Cancel)

Learning with Google Calendar

- **Organizational Skills and Time Management.** From an early age, children begin to experience the various pressures of time management with family, friends, conflicting events, and the idea of deadlines. The use of collaborative calendars is an easy way to help young people get a sense of time and events as they begin to see what is happening and what should happen across the various events of school, home, church, community, or other organizations to which they belong. With all this, they naturally begin to experience time conflicts and ask themselves the question: "What is the best use of my time right now?" Through the use of Google Calendars, adults can even begin to coach young people on how to set priorities and take responsibility for time management.

Resources

How to implement Google calendars
- http://video.google.com/videoplay?docid=-1918920791005482914#
- http://www.youtube.com/watch?v=2iTsxQFvQZQ

Chapter 12

Google Sites

Introduction

Google Sites is an excellent tool to create collaborative websites and share resources in a secure environment. It provides a very easy interface that allows for the insertion of all resources, including text, images, video, podcasts and forms. It also allows the documents you create in Google Docs or external documents such as a Word document to become part of a web page. Changes to documents displayed or linked to a Google Sites web page are automatically reflected on the web page. This feature is very popular with teachers. Google Sites can also serve as a wiki where multiple contributors can collaborate.

Getting Started

To create a website or wiki, locate the Google Sites link under the more tab at the top of your Gmail screen or search for Google Sites via a Google search.

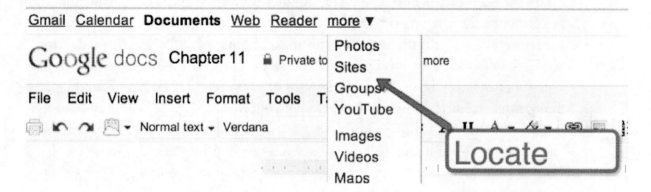

When you click into Sites, you'll get the following screen where you make a number of formatting choices, name your site or wiki, and get approval from Google.

After approval, you'll need to locate the various editing tools and controls at the top right side of the screen as pictured below. We suggest trying everything to get acquainted with how all the construction tools work. If you get stuck, search for some online tutorials.

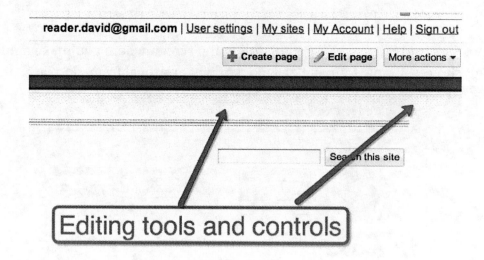

Advantages

Google Sites is much better than other website creation tools because it's:

- Instantaneous. Everyone can update the web page at the same time. In contrast, wikis lock editing to whoever requested access first. This lockout system is cumbersome because other users often have to wait minutes after the original editor has stopped editing to begin contributing.
- Large. Google Sites gives gigabytes as opposed to megabytes of storage space.
- Sustainable. Some smaller wiki companies have gone out of business leaving teachers with countless hours of work lost. Given their track record and the diversity of their business, Google is a good bet to stay in business for the long run.
- Free. Some wiki companies ask for money for extra features or include advertising as part of the cost of using their services. Google Sites is free and has no ads.

Sample Uses

- From our experience, most teachers do not need formal training on using Google Sites because the interface is very similar to a standard word processor. Below is a teacher's site that was completed over a period of two months. The science teacher that created this site taught herself how to use Google Sites. Notice that she has all courses set up on the left side and an assignment page. The School Logo on the top left is automatically created when new pages are created. The search feature at the top right is used all the time by students when looking for resources and is especially useful for those trying to find assignments.

- Google Sites has many useful features such as the filing cabinet web page which allows users to insert both Google Docs and external documents into one searchable web page. Notice below another example from a science teacher. This teacher especially loves this feature because he can put every course document (most of these documents were created before he started using Google Apps) on a web page. Below is an example of his chemistry web page with about 30 documents linked for this course. At the top right, students can search for any of these documents.

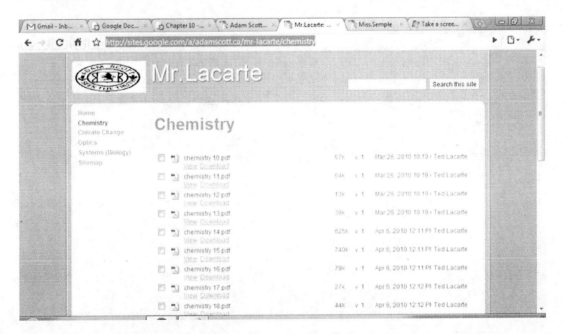

- Google Sites allows teachers to use pre-made templates or even to create their own. A school could create a template and allow teachers the option to use it. One major advantage of templates is that it gives each web page the same look and feel so that students or their parents have little problem navigating different teachers' web pages.

- Teachers could also create a web page for their students to use, thus giving them an organized collaborative virtual space. These templates make it easier for the entire class to navigate through each others' web spaces.

Learning with Google Sites

How can a web site or a wiki contribute to the teaching and learning going on in the classroom? A few major ideas come to mind:

- **Knowledge Building Centers.** In the examples shown previously, teachers are shown using a site as an organizational space for their students. In chapter five, we recommended that Google Sites be used as a knowledge building center: a place for a particular unit or learning experience where all the collaborative building, contributing, learning, working, exhibiting, and coaching are taking place. We gave the following example:

When a learning experience has a home, everyone has a central location that is familiar and welcoming for the collaborative work at hand. The impact on both teaching and learning need to be tracked in such an organized environment and reported out to interested administrators or used as examples of what quality teaching and learning "look like." Anyone can be allowed to view what is going on in real time, but only the actual participants can actually contribute, write, or edit. Re-read the description of knowledge building centers in chapter five for other ideas.

Here is a sample knowledge building center where the principal has challenged the students to come up with a plan to create a bully-free school:

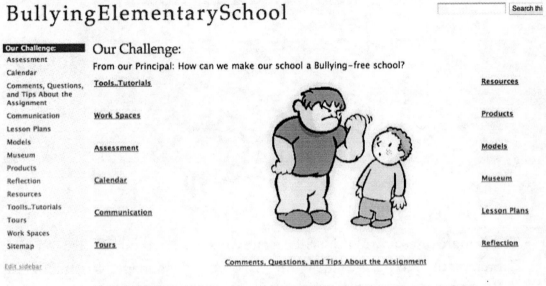

I

n a second example, students are working together on Internet safety:

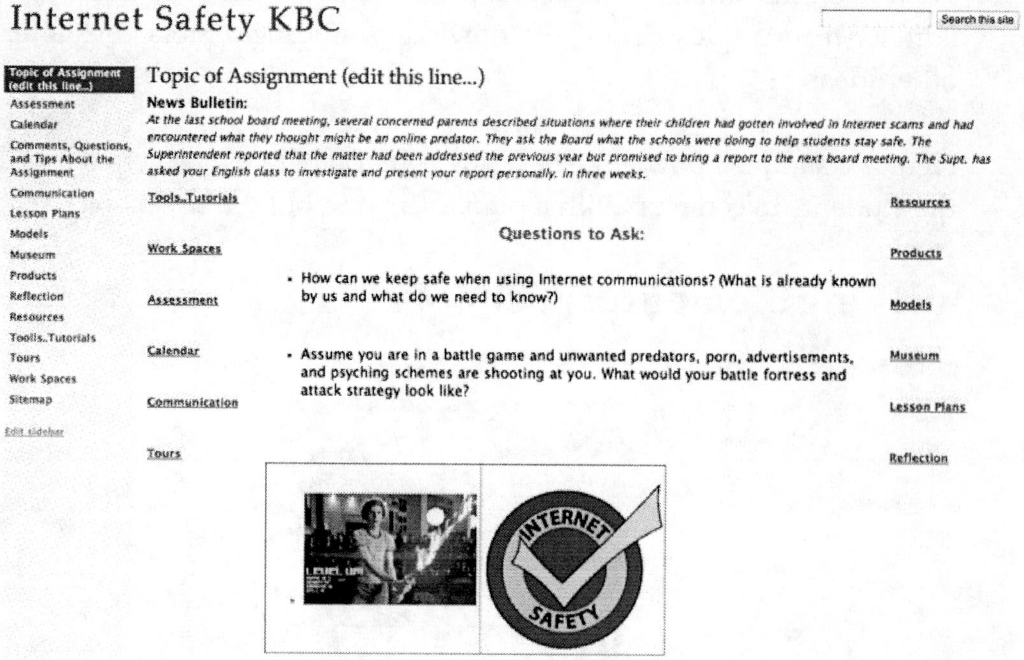

Internet Safety KBC

Search this site

Topic of Assignment (edit this line...)

Sidebar navigation:
- Topic of Assignment (edit this line...)
- Assessment
- Calendar
- Comments, Questions, and Tips About the Assignment
- Communication
- Lesson Plans
- Models
- Museum
- Products
- Reflection
- Resources
- Toolls..Tutorials
- Tours
- Work Spaces
- Sitemap

Edit sidebar

News Bulletin:
At the last school board meeting, several concerned parents described situations where their children had gotten involved in Internet scams and had encountered what they thought might be an online predator. They ask the Board what the schools were doing to help students stay safe. The Superintendent reported that the matter had been addressed the previous year but promised to bring a report to the next board meeting. The Supt. has asked your English class to investigate and present your report personally. in three weeks.

Tools..Tutorials

Work Spaces

Assessment

Calendar

Communication

Tours

Questions to Ask:

- How can we keep safe when using Internet communications? (What is already known by us and what do we need to know?)

- Assume you are in a battle game and unwanted predators, porn, advertisements, and psyching schemes are shooting at you. What would your battle fortress and attack strategy look like?

Resources

Products

Models

Museum

Lesson Plans

Reflection

- **Use Google Sites as a Wiki**. While a site can be used as a Knowledge Building Center, pieces and parts of the entire project can be managed by small groups using sites as an organizational wiki. For example, a small group might be investigating various aspects of World War II, so they set up a wiki within a Google Site as a place where they organize their work, embed websites, photos, or tools they can use, and report centrally on each person's progress. They also post links to documents being created as a research paper or a presentation that they are creating collaboratively. It becomes a home within the larger home of the Knowledge Building Center. Such a workspace can be monitored by the teacher, teacher librarian, technology teacher, or other specialist to see what progress is being made by each of the various groups. The wiki also provides a place where suggestions and coaching can happen. Various student groups can be asked to look at other group wikis to provide comments or see examples of how other groups are working. For example, if four groups were each taking a cultural aspect of a country and preparing reports of their assigned aspect, new groups could borrow from each of the wikis for the final construction of a cultural look at the country as a whole. Such uses of Google Sites as a project organization wiki helps in the actual construction and completion of projects that otherwise might languish without the structure.
- **Collaborative and individual knowledge construction.** Perhaps we have belabored this point to death, but a collaborative website constructed by students

and adults allows for the planning, construction, production, and exhibition of both individual and collective work. There are few technologies where both formative and summative assessments can be made and the progress of individuals and groups can be measured over time. Google Sites is fortunately one of these technologies. By simply having students "sign" their names to individual and group contributions, a search by student name will reveal each individual's contributions. This evidence combined with behaviors and other results done in face to face sessions in class, in the library, and as evidenced through group meetings and work sessions, combine as evidence of participation and quality of contribution. If parents, experts, specialists or even administrators in the school are coaching, editing, and contributing, then we are teaching and testing the impact of collaborative intelligence as a problem is solved or a project completed. When each and every participant knows that their work will be "public" then there is some motivation to put his or her best foot forward.

Selected Resources
- Google's Tutorial on how to create Sites http://sites.google.com/site/amslerclassroom/creating-a-new
- Google Help Page: http://www.google.com/support/sites/bin/static.py?hl=en&page=guide.cs&guide=23216&from=23216&rd=1
- Google Tutor helps you get started creating sites. http://www.googletutor.com/2008/05/29/getting-started-with-google-sites/

Chapter 13

Google Video

Introduction

Google Video allows users within the Google Apps domain to upload videos so anyone within the domain can view them. In other words, no one from the outside can view the videos inside your school's Google Apps for Education. Any video in wmv format (which is the standard format) can be uploaded. This would include videos from video cameras, flip cameras, and cell phones, along with videos created with Movie Maker, Photo Story and iMovie.

Getting Started

Google Video is included with Google Apps Education and does not need any special setup. All the administrator has to do is activate Google Video through the admin dashboard as pictured below from the administrator's screen:

M **Email**

http://mail.google.com/a/adamscott.ca

Calendar

http://www.google.com/calendar/hosted/adamscott.ca

Chat

Users can sign in by downloading Google Talk

Docs

http://docs.google.com/a/adamscott.ca

Sites

http://sites.google.com/a/adamscott.ca

Video

http://video.google.com/a/adamscott.ca

Selecting who has permission to upload Videos

Some students do not understand issues around privacy and content and we recommend that generally students should not be given permission to upload videos. Only teachers should give permission and they should view any video before it is put online.

When the administrator clicks on Video they can give permission to to up to 100 selected users to upload videos. The administrator's settings screen shot is illustrated below:

Video settings

Video Uploaders	Uploaders (up to 100, must be restricted to faculty and staff):

```
dougporter@adamscott.ca,
rogernevin@adamscott.ca,
ashwalker@adamscott.ca,
mrwright@adamscott.ca
```

Statistics　　Currently using **1.2 GB (11.7%)** of the (10.0) GB video quota

Users have uploaded 77 videos with a total length of 6.4 hours
Download top users by quota usage as CSV

Disable Video　　Disable Video
You can disable and remove this service without losing any data.

Video space is limited to 10 GB, which is about 60 hours of video. Administrators can generate a report which shows how much video space each user with permission to upload is using. The current usage can be seen in the settings screen above.

The administrator is also given the option to disable the video service without losing data. This may be done if there is inappropriate content online or if the Internet speed is slow. Video takes a lot of bandwidth and, by blocking it, it will speed up the other services.

Uploading a Video

Users who have permission to upload videos will be given the **video** tab at the top of their screen or may have to click on the **more** tab.

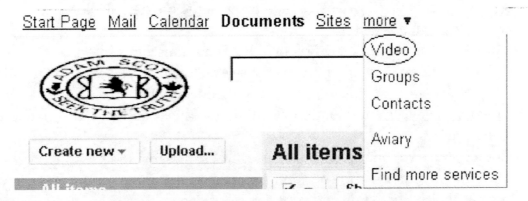

Next users will be given the following tabs. To upload they click on the upload tab and will then be able to browse their computer for the video file.

Home | **My Videos** | **Upload**

Showing 1 - 10 of about 77 for all videos visible to you

ENG 12 Oct 5 2010 Video
10/5/10 - 2 min 32 sec **rogernevin** Viewers: 2

Elizabeth's Video for Mr. Robert
Mr. Robert March 2010
3/29/10 - 3 min 6 sec **rogernevin** Viewers: 1

Tip: If the student wants to send the administrator or teacher a video, the best way to do it is to have the student upload the wmv file to their document area and share it with the administrator who can then review and post the video in the appropriate location. Email attachments don't work as well because of issues with large files.

Advantages

Google Video is better than other streaming video services because:
- It is free and contains no ads.
- Videos can only be accessed from within the domain with a login and password.
- Videos cannot be downloaded, which means users cannot distribute videos outside of the domain. This is different from YouTube where there are multiple sources to download videos and anyone posting on YouTube loses control of where their videos end up.
- Videos can only be uploaded by people the administrator selects.
- Privacy settings allow teachers to choose exactly who has access to the videos (everyone on the site, just one class or only one user).
- Videos can have a length of up to 60 minutes. This is better than YouTube's limit of 10 minutes.
- Google Video streams quickly because it uses the same tools as YouTube.
- The Administrator has the option to turn on or off certain tools with each video such as the ability to rate and comment on videos.

Sample Uses

- **Student-created projects** are probably the most common use of Google Video.
- **Field trip videos**. Remember that these videos can be private so that only the students, supervising adults, and parents can view.
- **Tutorials**. Students or adults can create tutorials that are easily uploaded and can save much orientation time to tools, procedures, school rules, etc.
- **Orientation videos** might be created to welcome students to the school, the learning commons, or other facilities or services.
- Students and adults can **promote** various programs within the school such as special courses, initiatives, fund raising events, etc.

Learning with Google Video

- Students are very engaged and tend to learn the content they are presenting. However, this is not automatic and so both content understanding and production quality need to be assessed.
- Creating videos appeals to many at-risk students because they may not be very good writers or readers, but they have the technical skills to produce good videos. They tend to take pride in their work when they see it on "film." For example, one student we know was bullied, so he created an anti-bullying video and showed it to many classes.
- Kids and teachers can rate and comment on videos using a five star rating. Better videos can be used as exemplars or even be used to teach certain concepts.
- Quick little videos using a program that comes with the purchase Smart Board called Smart Board Recorder is very useful in making demonstrations and tutorial videos. The program automatically records what is happening on the screen along with the ability to record voice and creates a video wmv file. For example, a math teacher can demonstrate how to solve an equation so it can be played over and over. The video is then uploaded to Google Apps Video where it can be viewed from any location, including the student's home.
- Record experimental strategies, talks, models, or demonstrations from professional development to be used by the faculty over and over.
- It is easy to put all the class project videos on to a web page so that they are all in the same space to be viewed and then archived as a group. This makes it very easy for the teacher to show all the students' videos by just clicking on them off one web page as opposed to getting videos emailed to them or brought in on memory sticks often in a format that will not work on the current media player. The resulting web page can be used as a list of examples of everyone's work. In addition, each of the videos can be rated and comments added.

Selected Resources

Photo Story Resources (Photo Story is an excellent free program for making simple videos from images and pictures. It is very popular in all subject areas from grades 2-12) http://tinyurl.com/3y9jfvr

Smart Board Recorder video http://tinyurl.com/dhxsww

Chapter 14

Google Start Page

Introduction

Each student and teacher in the enclosed space of Google Apps Education can have their own Start Page. This is the same idea as iGoogle, a product probably quite familiar to many of our readers. The essential concept is that your own Start Page is your way to control your information world, beginning with your academic life and extending into family, friends, hobbies, and the types of information and organizational tools you want instantly available to you when you log into your Google Apps account.

Description

Faced with a number of classes, projects, personal interests and preferences, the Start Page allows individuals to set up a Start Page that is a personal management area for their lives. Instead of facing the entire Internet, the user is creating a small subset of places to link to, projects, calendars and other management tools. The Start Page is a way to manage yourself in the world of information. It is your information space; your space to consume as well as work and enjoy. You can add the links and portals into whatever you need to stay organized. And, you can change that page as your information needs evolve, grow, or shrink. From this page, you access everything else you are working on and consuming.

Getting Started

First, the student creates their start page:

Second, the student adds various gadgets to their page including items for school, family, and fun:

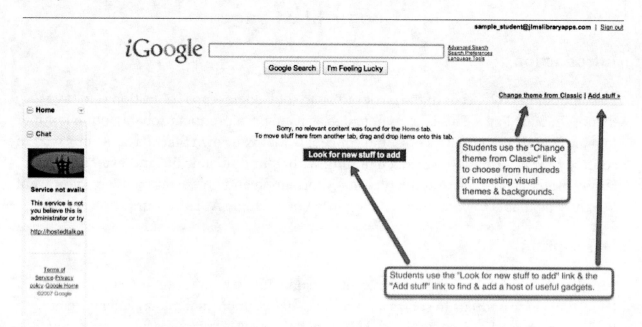

Ask students who already know how to create gadgets to teach the rest of the class how. Ask them to do demonstrations on the interactive white board. And, the result might look something like this:

Advantages

Like iGoogle, all kinds of benefits accrue to the individual who sets up an effective Start Page:

- The Start Page is a free personal organizer accessible on any computer, anytime, and anywhere, as long as you have an Internet connection.
- Each individual creates their own personal management of information space the way they want it organized.
- The Start Page is a one-stop place to access everything I am doing, consuming, or following at any given time, and it can be modified at any time. Thus, as my projects and assignments, including teachers, come and go, the Start Page is the place to add, modify, or delete access.
- It is a space where I can learn to manage myself within the blizzard of information and voices trying to grab my attention.

Sample Uses

- As teachers and students are introduced to the Google Apps for Education suite of tools, use teach one train one strategies or mass professional development with teachers and students to introduce the concept of the Start Page. Then as each teacher introduces a new topic or assignment, students add the appropriate link to their Start Page and they are off and running.
- Creating and maintaining a Start Page is a good time to think about Internet safety, digital citizenship, and the concept of coming into command of my own information space.
- Involve students in conceptualizing what it is they want to do in their individual Start Pages as they think about what they consume, their projects, and how to prevent unwanted intrusions on their space.
- Ask the teacher librarian or the teacher technologist to train a Geek squad in the school so that in most classes there will be a squad member who can give this instruction to the class.

Learning with Google Start Page

Constructing My Own Information space. What does it mean that we come into command of our own information spaces? What does it mean to regularly question who is trying to get my attention for what reasons and for what gain? The best creative minds in many businesses, governments, causes, and just plain nefarious individuals are doing their best to intrude on everyone's information space. We are bombarded and overwhelmed by messages and enticements. How do we all control this? And what is blocked from my access? Why? What skills do I need to avoid, reject, and ban voices from entering my space? As anyone begins to experiment with a Start page, the concept of what I want and don't want immediately becomes an issue; it is the time to learn to manage myself in information space; control what is pushed toward me, and immediately presents opportunities to manage school, family, and fun. Of course, this is much easier within Google Apps for Education because it is already within a protected space, but by starting here, I begin to handle a micro-world and that helps me as I build in that world of outer spaces known as the Internet.

Selected Resources

- Loertscher, David V. and Robin T. Williams. *In Command! Kids and Teens Build and Manage Their Own Information Spaces, And Learn to Manage Themselves in Those Spaces*. Hi Willow, 2008. ISBN 978-1933170-36-7. Available from http://lmcsource.com

Chapter 15

Google Apps for Education Mobile

Introduction

Google Apps for Education Mobile is available as part of the suite of tools within Google Apps for Education. Its purpose is to help students and teachers connect and work from an ever-growing list of mobile devices such as iPhones, BlackBerrys and Android phones. Users can also receive instant notifications of changes to their Google Apps for Education documents, sites and other productions in addition to utilizing Google Apps in an otherwise conventional fashion (i.e., on a laptop or desktop computer).

Such instant communication and collaboration from small, mobile devices is revolutionary as it allows teachers and students to work from not just anywhere with an Internet connection, but also anywhere with cellular service.

These mobile devices are also much more economical than their larger brethren, so the number of students possessing compatible mobile devices will certainly grow exponentially in the near future as will the services and products designed to work with them.

Getting Started

Google provides instructions on how to link various devices to Google Apps for Education. So, as shown below, find the link and then find the directions for the particular device you own.

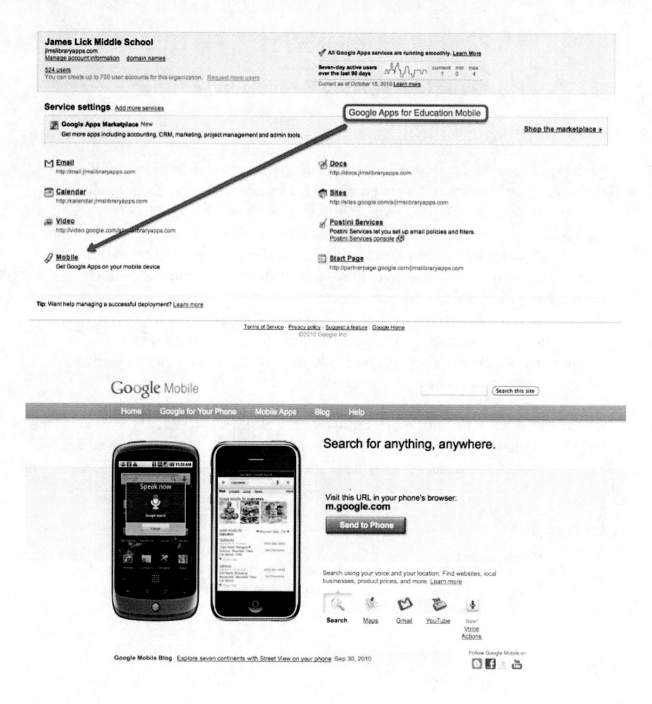

Probably the best approach to Mobile is to create various clubs in the school that have similar devices so that there is always a support group available. This could happen on a Google Site used as a wiki for various kinds of advice from everyone interested.

Chapter 16

Expanding the Utility of Google Apps
Google Apps Marketplace

Introduction

Adding to the practical functionality of Google Apps is Google Apps Marketplace. Google Apps Marketplace allows Google Apps administrators to add third-party products and services to users' accounts and to the wider domain as well.

While many of the services and products offered via Google Apps Marketplace are designed with the business world in mind, many are quite useful in educational settings, especially in the areas of productivity and organization. Examples of the latter are formLizard (which helps create and publish forms for public or in-house use), Noteilus (which syncs with the Google Apps Calendar to aid in note-taking and organization), and Aviary Design Tools (which provides powerful graphic tools and even allows users to create audio podcasts which are saved into Google Docs--an example is displayed below).

One of the great things about Google Apps Marketplace is that most of the products tie in directly with Google Apps and provide a cloud solution. If the administrator chooses a graphic program, both the program and the files created are in the cloud and are integrated into the other Google Apps. Any files created through an App like the Aviary Design Tools graphic editor or a podcasting tool are automatically saved in Google Docs.

Unlike most Google Apps, however, many of the products and services available through Google Apps Marketplace are not free. Subscriptions and outright purchases are required to fully utilize many. Shop, test, price, and evaluate the impact of the various allied tools for your own students' and teachers' needs.

Creating Your own Products to Enhance Communication and Collaboration

It is possible for a school or district to create its own customized products and applications that tie in with both the documents and communication tools of Google Apps. For example, if the district had the resources to hire an astute programmer, an online report card system could be developed that automatically updated as soon as teachers enter their marks. This system could even automatically email parents with the results.

Adding Third Party Products Through Marketplace

Only the Google Apps for Education administrator can add products by shopping Google Apps Marketplace through the Administration Dashboard by clicking "Shop the Marketplace." Many products in Google Apps Marketplace are free, including the aforementioned Aviary Design Tools.

Below is the screen where you can search Google Apps Marketplace. On the right side, there are the top rated products (with comments), on the left is a categorical list, and users are given an option to search by keyword.

Once a product is selected it will be shown on the Administrator Dashboard. As with other services, the Google Apps for Education administrator has control over the service. Below is a screen shot of the Aviary Design Tools service on the dashboard.

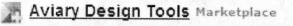

Once a product is active, users will be given the option to access it from the top tabs. They may have to choose **more** to make the selection.

In the example below, the user is given an option to use the following tools. Each of the tools will allow the user to save directly to Google Docs.

One of the most useful audio products available is the Edit Audio tool. This tool allows users to create and mix an audio podcast. The podcasts are saved and shared through Google Docs and can even be embedded into a web page.

Selected Resources

Video about using Google Apps Marketplace: http://tinyurl.com/yjpeel5

Official Google Apps Marketplace web page: http://www.google.com/enterprise/marketplace/

Chapter 17

Going Outside of Google Apps For Education

Introduction

Google has not included a number of its popular apps in the Education Edition package. But that keeps changing and gets better and better over time. So, if you want to take advantage of the many wonderful Web 2.0 tools out there, you have to take students outside of Google Apps Education to use them. And, when you are outside, all the rules and filters imposed by various tech directors and school policies apply.

Google Family Products Not in Google Apps for Education

While our list will be out of date the minute this book is distributed, the following family of general Google Apps is not currently a part of the Google Apps for Education Suite and cannot be accessed or used from within the suite. If you wanted to use these applications, you would have to exit Google Apps for Education entirely.

- **Maps:** maps, directions, and guidance getting you there
- **Picasa:** images and collections of images
- **Blogger:** blog your heart out
- **Draw:** simple drawing tools to create flow charts, diagrams, or models
- **Reader:** subscribe to various RSS and Atom feeds and view them on a single page
- **Images:** finding images across the web; many of which are copyrighted
- **Books:** search the contents of over ten million books and access them instantly
- **Translate:** find the right words in over 30 languages
- **Scholar:** search Google's bibliographic database to find peer-reviewed journal articles
- **Blogs** (not to be confused with Blogger): find the blogs you're looking for
- **Trends:** see what other people from around the world are using Google to find
- **Wonder Wheel:** see searches relevant to your own in graphical form
- **YouTube:** the short video world that changed everything. Google Video takes its place within Google Apps Education

Non-Google Products

A few of our favorites are listed below but there are hundreds of others to consider.

- **Jing (screen capturing tool):** capture screenshots and take video of whatever you can see on your screen, then use it to create tutorials, narrations or whatever you desire
- **Wall Wisher:** create a topic and have a conversation using multimedia stickies
- **Twitter** (& inserting Tweets into Google Apps Start-Up page): blog your heart out in 140 characters or less
- **Noodle Tools**: research software designed specifically for people like us: student, teacher and librarian researchers

In summary, the suite of tools available through Google Apps for Education can be widened by administrators on a case by case basis. We encourage those who decide to have not only a committee of adults who are thinking about these tools but also representative students who will have much to share. These student representatives can gather ideas from their peers and provide invaluable feedback to adults who will hopefully take their advice.

Part III

Administrative Concerns in Knowledge Building Environments

Chapter 18

Google Apps for Education Security

Introduction

Security is an important issue that is a challenge for administrators, IT directors, teacher librarians, teacher technologists, classroom teachers and students themselves. Just as in the physical world, a collaborative effort by all players is necessary to ensure safety in cyberspace. The purpose of this chapter is to give a few recommendations on how the integrated security system in Google Apps for Education operates. Currently, Postini is the security system provided free by Google to educational institutions.

For a Google Apps for Education administrator, a major priority should do be to:
- Check the policies of your district and the laws of your state and country about security issues. For example, in the U.S., the Children's Online Privacy Protection Act of 1998 (COPPA) rules must be followed by all schools receiving federal aid. In Ontario, Canada, schools are responsible for policing cyberbullying by any student, whether during the school day or at other times.
- Gain access to the Postini guidebook from Google via the Google Apps main site. Though we tried to cover here the most important parts of that document and the issues it brings to the implementing school, the more lengthy original document certainly warrants reading.
- Have all users and their parents or guardians sign Acceptable Use Policies.

Some things you should know about Postini:
- Postini and its services can be extended throughout other Google Apps and allows services within these tools to be turned on and off.
- Postini has features that allow for the filtering of such things as email and spam. Every day, the administrator receives a list of everything that was blocked within the last 24 hours. In our experience, this is fewer than ten items for a school with a thousand students. Postini even allows administrators to identify the offending student or adult if inappropriate messages are being sent.
- Postini allows different security levels for different groups or even different individuals. This means teachers could have more access to certain materials than students or older students could have slightly more access than their younger counterparts. Administrator can also create sub organizations and sub users.
- Various reports are available such as those detailing the use of different Google Apps tools.

- Postini will capture viruses that are sent to the system via attachment and tell you the account from which the virus came. Issuing accounts will be flagged.

Using Postini Security Services:

Postini can be found on the "administrators dashboard" and needs to be activated before it can be used. When you initially activate it, Google will send instructions on how to set your domain server to be in sync with the services. The activation is similar to activating email and should only take a few minutes to set up.

Postini service is broken down into two main modules: Message Center and System Administration.

The Message Center is rather straightforward and is the most common module used. It is responsible for filtering out Spam and other criteria-meeting emails before they are delivered. The administrator can read any email that is flagged in the Message Center and ascertain its worth before deciding whether to send it on to its intended recipient or to delete it. The Message Center, in combination with Gmail, also checks email attachments to see if they contain viruses.

The screen shot below shows the Message Center. Flagged email is placed in the "Junk" folder and the administrator can decide to deliver to email or put it into Trash.

The other main part of Postini is the System Administration module. It is very extensive and a comprehensive explanation is well beyond the scope of this book. Postini, in fact, comes with a detailed 412 page manual describing, among other things, how to do the following:

- Create and delete mass user accounts.
- Reconfigure mass user accounts. This would include turning services on or off for certain groups of students and changing passwords.
- Precisely control inbound and outbound email.
- Encrypt emails for security.
- Generate a wide variety of reports, including the usage of Google Apps, activity logs, and logs of any Spam and viruses intercepted.
- Set how much space users have for daily email and attachments.
- Create sub-domains of users each with different services and filters. For example, students and teachers could be set up as two sub domains with each having different access levels
- Specify what type of attachments can be delivered. For example, the administrator may not want students to be able to email executable attachments (often computer games) to each other.

The screen shot below shows the Administration Center.

What's Private and What's Not in Google Apps for Education?

The default in Google Apps is private for the owner (creator) of a document, but an owner can decide with whom to share a document. Owners of documents can even share their documents outside of their Google Apps for Education domain. That is, if the administrator has not disallowed it. The ability for Google Apps for Education to become a closed loop is crucial in dealing with privacy concerns.

Still, students using the Internet to access Google Apps may still access the cold, cruel world outside the managed domain—albeit not directly via Google Apps. For example, a URL for a YouTube video linked on a Google Sites page will still take the student to YouTube (barring school district filtering).

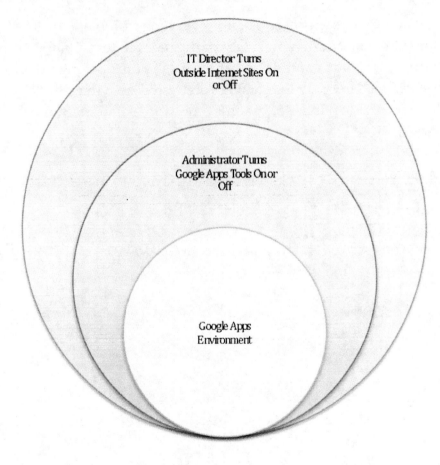

Other Security Issues

Start Page is a great place to teach kids to accept personal responsibility. Review the chapter in this book dealing with the Start Page, but it is something akin to an individual home page that allows the student to organize their lives and work. Building and managing a Start Page provides students an opportunity to hone their decision-making skills.

Security using student's personal devices. While it may take some doing to allow student personal devices on Google Apps, the same rules of access apply across devices whether they be home computers, laptops, tablets, smart phones, etc..

The Google Apps system is very friendly to a wide variety of devices such as netbooks and Macs. Future operating systems may sync personal computers while on the cloud, but store documents on the personal computing device simultaneously. This would be similar to iTunes and audio book companies that allow documents to be worked on when no Internet access is available, but to also sync to the cloud when later connected.

Perhaps our best advice for security is that it is everyone's problem. Instead of one person "in command," the entire community participates in formulating both individual controls and group controls and at the same time opening up opportunities as wide as possible. It is very easy to imagine what could go wrong, but as in the physical world, we provide public spaces and concentrate on individual offenders. The group spaces are "policed" by everyone.

Selected Resources

Video on Google Apps security http://tinyurl.com/3zxsb3

Chapter 19

Google Apps for Education and Administrators

School administrators hold the key to the successful adoption and implementation of Google Apps for Education. It is not just a matter of signing various forms and opening the gate, it's part of an entire school improvement plan that places technology in a position to affect the quality of teaching and learning. It's a part of a plan to connect with students in a world where they feel comfortable and where they flourish. It's embracing a world in which young people are developing digital citizenship and learning how to cope with the dangers associated with both physical spaces and cyberspace. It is about coaching kids and teachers to learn in an atmosphere of positive enhancements, rather than governing from fear.

In this chapter we cover some of the issues facing school administrators and we cover potential talking points useful in justifying a teaching and learning role for technology in the school.

It's a Fact:

To register Google App Education Edition you must get the approval of your school's administration. Google requires a school administrator to sign the documents as part of the registration.

Its Also a Fact:

A myriad of issues surround the opening of a new computer environment to both faculty and students. Every school administrator must launch that new environment with a purpose and a determination to adopt a major change. It's not just a matter of simply switching from paper to digital. The changes are far more dramatic as both adults and learners switch centuries and 180 degree thinking, planning, doing, and assessing. It is a whole new world.

The central negative arguments against moving toward any environment such as Google Apps for Education usually center around fear and the loss of control by the IT staff. Thus, our first recommendation to school administrators considering the signing of a Google Apps for Eduction form: **Talk to administrators in other schools who have successfully implemented the system over a period of time**. Another great practice is to take the technology leadership team to a district where the system has been successfully launched and ask questions: How does it work? What opportunities has it opened up? What were the major challenges and how were they overcome? And, above all, try to ascertain the impact on teaching and learning.

Arguments to be made in favor of Google Apps for Education

"Google Apps has worked out better than I could have ever imagined. We expected a more reliable, stable, and virus-free email. But we got more—a suite of integrated collaborative applications that are being used by teachers and in our classrooms. " Scott Graden, Superintendent, Saline Area Schools (Saline, MI, USA).

- Millions of students around the world use it, including Arizona State University, University of Southern California, and public school students in the states of Oregon, Colorado and New York.
- Google Apps is SECURE and protects privacy with industry standard tools such as Postini.
- Google Apps saves thousands, if not millions, of dollars. It is FREE!
- Google Apps allows the school to concentrate funding for technology by putting resources towards increasing bandwidth and wireless connections rather than on server space and expensive commercial district-owned applications since all information is stored in the CLOUD.
- Using Google Apps for Education is a giant leap toward EQUITY since it is available from most computing devices anywhere and at any time.
- Google Apps allows students to connect with their own devices, which takes the stress off school computers and allows more access.
- Google Apps gives students access to a plethora of free applications for use anytime, anywhere.

Hint:

- Expect any administrator or school board member to expect to receive a proposal for Google Apps for Education. In such a proposal, include relevant research articles, links and examples of Google Success Stories. See http://getgoogleapps.com for online resources, testimonials, and an introduction to Google Apps for Education (featuring a principal).
- Arrange a Skype or Google Talk live session with a successful administrator and IT director to verify that the above statements are correct.

Contributions to Teaching and Learning

- Google Apps for Education improves learning by allowing students and teacher to work more productively and giving 24/7 access.
- Google Apps allows for collaborative based group projects which research shows is the best type of learning.

- Google Apps allows students and teachers to create knowledge building centers. A great example of this is the Virtual War Museum web site created using Google Sites where groups of students collaborate to create different virtual museum rooms. The museum is an on-going assignment where students for each semester add to the museum.
- Google Apps engages students by using the same type of social networking tools that students use in their personal lives. While working on shared documents students will also use the chat feature to make side comments as they work.
- Google Apps allows students to do assignments they would have been impossible without a cloud paradigm. A good example is the grade 9 Geography teacher who now can point to a group of students in their class and tell them to create a virtual collaborative presentation and post it to a web page. The cloud allows students to work on ONE document using the same software from remote locations.
- Google Apps puts students in an environment of 21st Century skills.
- Google Apps for Education improves communication between students, teachers and other specialists in the school. A collaborative environment is a natural result of the structure of the environment itself.

Other General Benefits to the School:

- Google Apps for Education provides great communication tools with parents and the school community.
- Google Apps gives all users a shared virtual presence.
- Google Apps promotes the school as being progressive, although we predict that within five years, this and other systems will be commonplace.
- Google Apps is good for the environment by making a paperless environment a natural and normal expectation because of communication, document sharing, and collaborative work in digital space.
- Google Apps for Education is based on research and best practices. (See the 2009 Horizon Report.)

The Follow Through

While school administrators might be impressed with our pitch and rosy pictures of potential benefits, their critical support is needed for the sustainability of the Google Apps for Education initiative. The technology leadership team should have a plan in place to document progress as well as to assess the impact of the implementation. Below is a list of program elements that school administrators might want to monitor. Add and modify the list for your own school or district:

- Progress of installation of the system

- Progress of initial training of the first wave of teacher implementers
- Progress of training for a student tech team to assist in the school-wide training
- Reports from early adopters and the students involved
- Development of model learning experiences that have had an impact on learning
- Report of less-successful implementations and plans for their improvement
- Timeliness for launch to a wider body of the faculty and student body
- Results of wider professional development activities
- Monitoring of the individual learning experiences and their impact on teaching and learning
- Development of new Google features or expansion of the initial Google Apps for Education component parts

One of the best ways school administrators can be involved is to include them in the various Knowledge Building Centers where actual learning experiences are taking place. They are free to lurk, but can also be valuable experts and consultants at critical points during the event. School administrators should understand that this is an excellent way to do "walk-throughs" of classrooms whether they be online classes or face-to-face experiences.

Selected Resources

- Testimonials and case studies of schools you Google Apps: http://www.google.com/a/help/intl/en/edu/customers.html
- Seven things you should know about Google App: http://tinyurl.com/6a4775
- 2009 Horizon Report: http://www.nmc.org/pdf/2009-Horizon-Report.pdf

Chapter 20

Getting Started with Google Apps for Education

Google Apps Education Edition is free for non-profit schools. To register there are three main steps:

1. get permission from an administrator
2. purchase a domain name, and
3. fill in the online form at www.google.com/a/edu. Registration may take around six weeks.

Administrator permission

To register Google Apps Education you must first get approval from your school's administrators. (See Chapter 19 on tips for how to promote the use of Google Apps with school administrators.) Once you convince your school administrators, you will find all the necessary information from the Google Apps for Education web site: http://www.google.com/a/help/intl/en/edu.

Domain Name:

A domain name, such as jeffersonhigh.org, can be purchased for around $15 USD from a domain registry company such as godaddy.com. The domain that you purchase will become the web address that will be used for all your Google Apps for Education services.

The domain you register will redirect or forward users from the domain address to your Google Apps web address. For example, Adam Scott Collegiate and Vocational School's Google Apps web address (purchased domain) is http://adamscott.ca. When users type this address into a browser, they are redirected to https://www.google.com/a/adamscott.ca. Although you must pay to register and maintain the domain, you do not have to pay for web space because all your web space and services is provided by Google.

When you purchase a domain address make sure you can access and edit MX records. To use the email under your domain name you must change the MX records. This sounds complicated, but isn't and usually only takes a couple of minutes. Google provides a short video on how to do this (follow the links at getgoogleapps.com to see the video).

Many schools already have a domain and a web page that they have probably used for years. You could also use this domain for Google Apps, but you would have to migrate all the web pages over to Google Sites. This could prove to be a daunting task. More often, it is simpler to just purchase a separate domain address that is used exclusively for Google Apps. If Google Apps is purchased on the school district level and they have the resources, then the migration of web pages may very well be the best option.

The Administration Dashboard

All administration is done using the Administrative Dashboard and is accessed by logging in and clicking on your Gmail at the top left. Then, when you are able to see your Gmail screen, click on "Manage this domain," near the top middle.

When you first log in, you will notice that not all services are active. Some are turned on by just clicking on them, while others such as Gmail and Postini need some technical changes on your domain server (see web links below).

Screen Shot of Administration Dashboard

Service settings Add more services

> **Google Apps Marketplace** New
> Get more apps including accounting, CRM, marketing, project management and admin tools.
> Sho

Email
http://mail.google.com/a/adamscott.ca

Docs
http://docs.google.com/a/adamscott.ca

Calendar
http://www.google.com/calendar/hosted/adamscott.ca

Sites
http://sites.google.com/a/adamscott.ca

Chat
Users can sign in by downloading Google Talk

Video
http://video.google.com/a/adamscott.ca

Postini Services
Postini Services let you set up email policies and filters.
Postini Services console

Mobile
Get Google Apps on your mobile device

Start Page
http://partnerpage.google.com/adamscott.ca

Contacts beta
http://www.google.com/contacts/a/adamscott.ca

Groups (user-managed)
http://groups.google.com/a/adamscott.ca

Short Links Google Labs
http://engagestudents.ca.adamscott.ca
http://shortlinks.adamscott.ca

Creating User Accounts

Once you get confirmation from Google, you create users either individually or all at once from a text file with students' names, user names and passwords.

Your school administration should have access to student text files which you can use to create a file that will automatically create all users at once in a batch. We recommend using an MS Excel or Open Office spreadsheet to manipulate the text files you receive from administration. Your final file will contain the data shown below with each field separated by a comma (comma separated value). Once the file is created go to the Administrative Dashboard and click on "Advanced Tools" and choose "Bulk Upload." It will take about 10 minutes to an hour before all user accounts are created.

From Google Web Site:

Make a list of user accounts

You'll need to create a CSV (comma separated value) file with the user account information. Spreadsheet programs including Google Docs and Microsoft Excel make it easy to create and edit CSV files.

Your CSV file should be formatted as a table and must include a header, or first line, that defines the fields in your table. The headers should be: email address, first name, last name, password. Example:

	A	B	C	D
1	email address	first name	last name	password
2	picasso@adamscott.ca	Pablo	Picasso	59h731
3	claude.monet@adamscott.ca	Claude	Monet	6d8945
4	lilies@adamscott.ca	Georgia	O'Keeffe	319w56

Setting Up Email

To activate email you need to change the MX records on you web page domain. See Resource Links below to do this. Users will receive an email address with a combination of their login and the domain (johnsmith@jeffersonhigh.org). As an administrator you can turn off access to any services at any time, so students who misuse the system could lose their email privileges.

Introducing Google Apps for Education into a School.

Generally, we find students learn how to use Google Apps quicker than teachers, which is great because teachers can take advantage of student knowledge if they are having problems with Google Apps themselves.

We find the best way to introduce Google Apps is to start with Google Docs and Google Sites. We give students a short activity where they have to to log in to Google Apps, create a document with images, and create a web page with video. Both the document and the web site have to be shared. A copy of this assignment with a rubric are at the back of this book.

It is very important when Google Apps is introduced that students be told very clearly not to use any of the services such as email or chat for personal communication. Almost all students will understand this and you should have few problems with misuse of the system.

It is better to start small and have success than trying to implement Google Apps quickly through a large school where there are inadequate resources. Many teachers will try a new technology once, but if they are met with anything but success, they are very hesitant to try it again. As you build your success stories, other teachers will ask to be part of Google Apps.

Selected Resources

Video Tutorial on how to edit MX records to activate email http://tinyurl.com/9mg7d5

Part IV

Onward!

Chapter 21

Keeping Up / Conclusion

As with any evolving product (or perpetual beta product as many such software applications are known), keeping up with Google Apps for Education is a constant process. We recommend that everyone in your community of learners take responsibility to keep up and spread the word about changes and new opportunities. It's all a part of a collaborative community where I teach you, you teach me, and we all learn together. In our final chapter, we provide just a few hints and examples of what you find out when hooked into the Google Apps community.

Official Sources

- Start with the official Google Apps for Education site at:
  http://www.google.com/a/edu
- To register your school for Google Apps for Education, go here:
  http://www.google.com/a/help/intl/en/edu/index.html
- To collaborate with other educators and get Google Apps for Education news:
  http://www.google.com/educators/index.html
- Sample units of instruction using the suite of tools:
  http://www.google.com/a/help/intl/en/edu/lesson_plans.html
- Connect with Google certified trainers:
  http://sites.google.com/site/gtaresources/gct-pages
- News: http://www.google.com/educators/index.html
- For helps, news and announcements. Check out the Google Apps Education Community: http://edu.googleapps.com
- Google Teacher Academy: http://www.google.com/educators/gta.html
- More tutorials and tips: http://edu.googleapps.com/tutorials-and-tips
- Google booths at various conferences such as ISTE.

If interested, you can affiliate with Google formally in several major opportunities such as:

- **Google Apps for Education Certified Trainer program**. If you are already an expert on Google Apps, you may be interested in applying to be a Google Apps for Education Certified Trainer to deliver professional development to schools. Certified Trainers will be listed on the Google Apps for Education site and in the Google Apps Marketplace. Requirements include passing a set of 6 paid exams based on content in the Google Apps for Education Training Center (http://edutraining.googleapps.com). For more information and the full application, please review: http://www.google.com/apps/teachertraining

- **Google Apps for Education Certified Trainer Summits**. Those applying for the Certified Trainer program may also be able to attend a Certified Trainer summit. Spots are limited for these summits, so you must apply to the Certified Trainer program and, in the application, provide information about a session you would like to lead: http://www.google.com/apps/teachertraining

Unofficial Sources

A Google search will turn up all types of helpful sites that provide various helps. For example, check out http://www.learnitin5.com for a series of videos on Web 2.0 tools and techniques that can be used in the classroom. These videos can be used as models for students needing to create video tutorials on tools others in class need.

Check out various blogs. Just one sample:
- Lisa Thumann is an excellent blogger and can keep you informed about may tips and tricks with the broader world of Google Apps and technology in education. See her blog at: http://thumannresources.com

The Extension to This Book

As a reminder, check out the extensions of this book to learn of new ideas and updates plus an opportunity to participate in discussions:
- Website: http://getgoogleapps.com
- Facebook page: http://www.facebook.com/GoogleAppsForEdBuildingKnowledge

Conclusion

The technological advances that have taken place in the past few decades have provided today's teachers and students with both opportunities and challenges. Most of today's teachers belong to a generation fortunate enough to have watched technological advancements grow by unbelievable leaps and bounds.

Today's students, however, have seen little such change in their lives. Unlike their teachers, their challenge is not so much to adapt to the changing, increasingly digital world around them, but rather to learn in an industrial model educational system still employing analog tools. If these students are to be expected to compete in the global marketplace of ideas, their educational system and their teachers have to catch up with the times and, most importantly, its students.

Collaborative learning technologies like Google Apps allow teachers and students to work together like never before. Through the increased incorporation of Google Docs and other Web 2.0 technologies into curriculum, both students and teachers can begin to master the tools and skills they will need to continue to excel in the future.

The combination of Google Apps, open wireless, and portable computer labs using netbooks is an exciting new model that can enhance the learning and creative opportunities for students at a lower cost and more secure environment of any system we have seen to date. It just keeps getting better and better.

Appendix A

New Additions to Google Apps for Education

As authors, it became a joke among us that we had authored a book with the shortest life span ever. Thus, we added Appendix A to try to keep up with a speeding bullet.

In an announcement late Nov. 2010, Google initiated the following massive release of new tools in the Google Apps for Education suite. Here is the official list as announced at: https://sites.google.com/site/gaeservices/ We have produced their master list below with commentary of our own about the various tools and longer commentary for the most important ones.

In addition, during the first week of Dec. 2010, Google announced Google eBooks that competes directly with Amazon's Kindle initiative. Both provide digital books on a variety of ereaders and other devices but have not dealt with the institutions such as schools and libraries, preferring instead, to go directly to the customer. This means that much will change in the world of digital textbooks and other information sources in the coming few years. Readers are advised to try to keep up not only with the various new devices but also information access - access to quality information and multimedia, that is. And, the technologies place the learner not only in an information consuming world but in the world of creating content in an amazing array of technologies and mediums. Much of this new content can be circulated within the safe environment of Google Apps for Education rather than competing with the vast ocean out in the Internet as a whole. Here is the annotated list of new tools:

Alerts

Receive news and search results via email (example: a student or teacher wants to receive daily notices of any topics added to the web on a particular topic that is being researched. Google will send you an email every day with the links to sites that include the topic you are interested in receiving. You can stop the topical search results at any time. Thus, if a project lasted several weeks or longer, this tool would help the student receive some of the latest information available on the web.)

Blog Search

Find blogs on your favorite topics (example, if you want to build a personal learning network on a favorite topic, a search of who is blogging on that topic can be conducted from time to time. By examining the various blogs on the topic, you can choose those you want to follow on a regular basis. Older children and teens are not too young to learn to develop their own personal learning network (PLN). It can begin in their hobbies such as following sports figures or commentators or avocations such as dinosaurs or hot air balloons. It is an opportunity for young people to experience what expertise looks like and for adults to encourage in-depth explorations and deep understanding.)

Google Books and Google ebooks

Search the full text of books (The Google Books initiative has been scanning millions of books in libraries and makes those available for free or fee depending on copyright restrictions. Now, Google is going into the sale of eBooks that are available with many types of eBook readers and mobile devices such as the Kindle, iPad, or Androide devices. This has huge implications for the textbook industry and libraries. The major test of the next few years will be where digital information will reside: on your own device or in the cloud or both. For students, digital textbooks and connections to all types of digital content on any device and at any time or place will be a major challenge for all schools and parents.)

Google Chrome

A browser built for speed, stability and security (The choice of one browser over another is a matter of personal choice, but also subject to whether any particular web site has been created to work well under a variety of browsers. Young people might have a regular favorite, but should be prepared to use a variety of browsers and search engines. Google has also announce the Google Chrome Gingerbread operating system that will be rolled out in 2011 and will have major implications for access to the Web and to digital content of all types.)

Desktop

Search your own computer (Opening this App to learners opens up the world of gadget creation. See the tutorial at: http://code.google.com/apis/desktop/docs/Tutorials/ ModifyHelloWorld/index.html#1 or you can easily search for a video tutorial such as: http://www.top-windows-tutorials.com/google-desktop.html Warning! introducing such tools to young people just may infect them with not only a new hobby but push them toward a technology career.)

Directory

Browse the web by topic (Like Wikipedia, Google solicits volunteers to help "catalog" the web. Each volunteer can select a topic and then assist the search engine in identifying the best sites. Some of the young people we teach have in-depth knowledge of some topics to volunteer for such a role. Some teachers like Richard Byrne of the Free Technology for Teachers blog might also contribute their considerable knowledge to help.)

Earth

Explore the world from your PC (Google Earth is one of the most popular of all the Google Apps and is probably known by many of the student's family and even extended family. Amazing views of almost anywhere on Earth can be accessed - even views of underneath the Ocean. Now, students have access to this amazing tool that touches almost every discipline taught in K-12 education. In the next edition of this book, we will devote an entire chapter to this tool and learning opportunities connected to it. In the meantime, there are hundreds of examples on the Web and in print for using Google Earth. It is a major addition to this suite of tools.)

Google Finance

Business info, news, and interactive charts (Could be useful to economics and business classes in high school.)

Images

Search for images on the web (millions of images can be location; many of inferior quality and clarity and usefulness. Many of these images are under copyright and should be used under the fair use provisions of the copyright law. Students are advised to use the Creative Commons source of images where the use in spelled out. However, the prospect of student-created images that are accessible by everyone in the school holds high appeal as both kids and teachers share all types of visual images of the real or imaginary world for use in the curriculum. Check out Google Picassa to do this.)

Maps

View maps and directions (Looking up street addresses and finding routes to places is not only an immediate need satisfied by maps, but valuable for Geography projects such as state reports, world reports, or local study.)

News

Search thousands of news stories (Obviously valuable for contemporary issues, students can get quick links to national and international news and can search the news stories to follow topics.)

Scholar

Search scholarly papers (Worth a search by students. Scholarly articles and books may be excerpts or full text depending on the copyright of the original. Often the student can connect in with the local academic library that might have the item. Most students would probably prefer to use the school's online databases for instant access to topical research, but if those searches fail, then this might provide some assistance.)

Toolbar

Add a search box to your browser (On either Mac or PC, a toolbar can be added to Google just below the main toolbar that gives instant access to a wide variety of apps and shortcuts. Since these change often, check out the current list and add them to several computers to see whether they are of value to users. This could be another assignment for the Geek Squad to investigate and recommend to teachers, other students, and to the administrator of Google Apps for Education.)

Trends

Explore past and present search trends (Want to know what folks are searching Google on a specific day? Trends provides the top most popular searches being done. This might return such mundane things as school closings in Syracuse NY during a snowstorm, death of a celebrity, or advice on a current health problem. One can search any day back as far as 1997 to watch interest on the web.)

Web Search

Search billions of web pages, and, Web Search Features
Do more with search (Students and teachers almost always overestimate their ability to search the Web, whether doing a Google search or any other type of search. Teacher librarians should be expert searchers on a variety of search engines and teach these skills to both teachers and students as a normal part of accessing information. As students become better and better searchers themselves, they could create tutorials for their fellow classmates about doing searches for specific projects. Involving students in

this way solidifies a skill and at the same time, helps them and others locate quality information for topics being researched.)

Explore and innovate

Code

Developer tools, APPs and resources (For students who are getting serious about careers in technology and programming, here is an App to get them started at a level where they can work with actual program development at the writing code level.)

Labs

Try out new Google products (For the school Geek Squad, interest can be maintained by having them try and test new Apps or software programs for consideration by the rest of the school. Google is always looking for testers of beta Apps. It is a great way to help keep the adults in a school informed about what is coming down the pike and what might be worth teaching to the rest of the school. We have commented elsewhere on the value of student participation in creating, maintaining, operating, and teaching various systems within the Google Apps for Education family. It is better to have kids on your side than having them be hackers.)

Communicate, show & share

Blogger

Express yourself online (At last, students have the opportunity in the Google Apps for Education family of using a blog that is safe and secure. Blogging, or the keeping of personal journals or commentaty are extremely useful in education. Almost any class in the school can profit by using blogs on which students can log, report, reflect, share, or comment about whatever they are working on. Teachers or fellow students can comment on a particular blog and access can be as closed or open as needed. Many educational authors have offered uses for blogs in the classrooms as a part of projects and even assessment of what is known. In our next edition of this book, we will devote an entire chapter to the uses of blogs in the classroom and to promote both deep understanding and 21st century skills.)

Groups

Create mailing lists and discussion groups (Any number of students or teachers can create an easy group to communicate and share with by creating a Google Group. For example, if students in the the U.S. were doing a project with a group in Brazil, they might set up a Google Group to facilitate communication within a Knowledge Building Center as they try to solve problems, share information, or do projects together. Only group members can share and communicate so privacy is a great advantage for the group.)

Orkut

Meet new people and stay in touch with friends (Google's version of Facebook is used most often by developers creating gadgets or doing other projects. Experimentation by students in project creation and organization is worth investigating.)

Picasa

Find, edit and share your photos (Like iPhoto, students can use their mobile phones/ cameras to take, download, and then create photo galleries. Picasa makes these photo galleries public or private making the study of the current community, school, vacationing, or current events fodder for all kinds of projects and assignments. And, don't forget the world of micro photography for students studying science.)

SketchUp

Build 3D models quickly and easily (A great tool to create quick drawings or elaborate models to illustrate objects or even ideas. For example, a building can be found in Google Earth and then imported into SketchUp and then using the drawing tools, a 3D model can be developed. This model can then be sent to Google for approval and can then enter their gallery of 3D models from all over the world. A wonderful way to introduce kids of all ages to the world of drawings, models, and sketches that can be used in almost any area of study.)

Talk

IM and call your friends through your computer (Along side the Gmail screen, one can install Google Talk. Instantly, you see a list of your contacts who can be chatted with or who have video connections so you can video chat. If the person's name is green, it means they are currently on line. If gray, they are not on line. So, it is very convenient to establish either text messaging or a video chat while in the email program. This feature is helpful to students collaborating day or night on various projects and assignments.)

Translate

View web pages in other languages (depending on the language, one can translate foreign language websites or messages. The translations are not very good, but would be valuable in multiple language classrooms or in foreign language courses. Google has a program soliciting volunteers to help make the translations more accurate. This feature could easily become a project of a class of multilingual students.)

YouTube

Watch, upload and share videos (Google Video allows an internal school video library to be developed by teacher and students; the administrator can also turn on or off access to the full YouTube in the outside world.)

Make your computer work better

Pack

A free collection of essential software (Instead of having to download the various Google Apps one at a time, this program allows students or teachers to download a group of Apps all at once on to their personal computers. It's a time saver.)

About the Authors

Roger Nevin is currently a teacher-librarian at Adam Scott C.V.I. in Peterborough Ontario, Canada. He has successfully implemented Google Apps for Education into schools through the school library and sees it as a vital tool that greatly improves learning and engages students through knowledge based virtual collaboration. Roger is president of the Ontario School Library Association (2011), is founder of three non-profit educational web sites: engagestudents.ca, connectingeducation.com and boysread.com, and has presented at numerous conferences.
You can contact Roger at:
rnevin@gmail.com
twitter.com/rogernevin

Micah Melton lives in San Francisco, California and works as a Teacher Librarian for the San Francisco Unified School District. He holds a M.L.I.S. from San Jose State University, a M.A. in Education from the University of San Francisco, and a M.Ed. in History from Southwestern Oklahoma State University. Micah first started using Google Apps in 2006 while looking for a means to store his students' documents. The collaborations that followed changed the nature and quality of his and other teachers' students' writing, and quickly altered the way many curricular projects are completed throughout the San Francisco Unified School District.
You can contact Micah at:
mr.m.melton@gmail.com
meltonm@sfusd.edu

David Loertscher is a professor of library and information science at San Jose State University in California and has written and presented internationally on a wide variety of topics connected to education and most recently the development of the learning commons in schools. His interest in Google Apps was kindled the first time he experienced the idea in both the spreadsheet and documents where collaborative work could be done. That innovation for teaching and learning has flowered into the use of many Web 2.0 tools and the development of knowledge building centers.
You can contact David at:
reader.david@gmail.com
twitter.com/davidloertscher
http://davidvl.org
http://schoollearningcommons.pbworks.com

How this Book was Written

This book was written by Roger Nevin, Micah Melton and David Loertscher almost exclusively via Google Docs. The use of Google Apps allowed the authors to work collaboratively in real time on the same documents though thousands of miles apart.

We assigned principal responsibilities for some chapters using colors to designate who was writing what. Then all had a chance to edit the chapters before going to Rebecca Brodegard for final editing and layout. Rebecca used Pages from the iWork Suite to do the layout and Mark Loertscher translated the Pages file into the ebook format for uploading to the various aggregators. The book is available both in print and as an ebook for Kindle, the Nook, and various other devices. At this point in time, ebook formats require simple in-line text and illustrations, so no fancy layout for the printed book was planned since that would require doing the editing and layout twice.

One interesting experience was using Goolge Call Phone to link Roger from Canada and David in Utah on a lengthy telephone call during which we worked simultaneously on four chapters. Sometimes one dictated to the other who was writing, sometimes both were writing and editing the chapter simultaneously. The entire book has been an amazing collaborative experience as we relied on what each other knew or could discover about Google Apps for Education and combining our collective experience and knowledge.

Simply put, this book project would not have been possible without the tools Google Apps provides.

Finally, the web page and Facebook page that accompanies this book provide an opportunity for wider discussion and updating on a tool that is constantly evolving.

Index